The Berkeleys

neighbors

Molly Elliot Seawell

Alpha Editions

This edition published in 2024

ISBN : 9789367240632

Design and Setting By
Alpha Editions
www.alphaedis.com
Email - info@alphaedis.com

As per information held with us this book is in Public Domain.
This book is a reproduction of an important historical work. Alpha Editions uses the best technology to reproduce historical work in the same manner it was first published to preserve its original nature. Any marks or number seen are left intentionally to preserve its true form.

Contents

CHAPTER I. .... - 1 -

CHAPTER II. .... - 12 -

CHAPTER III. .... - 20 -

CHAPTER IV. .... - 28 -

CHAPTER V. .... - 33 -

CHAPTER VI. .... - 37 -

CHAPTER VII. .... - 44 -

CHAPTER VIII. .... - 49 -

CHAPTER IX. .... - 58 -

CHAPTER X. .... - 65 -

CHAPTER XI. .... - 72 -

CHAPTER XII. .... - 79 -

CHAPTER XIII. .... - 83 -

CHAPTER XIV. .... - 88 -

CHAPTER XV..- 95 -

CHAPTER XVI. ....- 103 -

CHAPTER XVII..- 108 -

CHAPTER XVIII..- 123 -

CHAPTER XIX. ....- 130 -

CHAPTER I.

A PROVINCIAL Virginia race-course is an excellent place to observe a people which has preserved its distinctiveness as well as the Virginians. So far, they have escaped that general and fatiguing likeness which prevails in most of the universe these days.

Therefore, the Campdown race-course, on a golden day in October, looked like itself and nothing else. The track had started out with the intention of making a perfect ellipse, but meeting a steep incline, it saved the trouble of bringing up the grade, by boldly avoiding the obstacle—so the winning post was considerably nearer the half-mile than the starting post was. Nobody objected to a little thing like this, though. The Virginians are good-natured creatures, and seldom bother about trifles.

It was the fall meeting of the Campdown Jockey Club—a famous institution "befo' the war."

At this time the great awakening had not come—the war was not long over. For these people, had they but known it, the end of the war really meant the end of the world—but the change was too stupendous for any human mind to grasp all at once. There came a period of shock before the pain was felt, when the people, groping amid the ruins of their social fabric, patched it up a little here and a little there. They resumed in a dazed and incomplete way their old amusements, their old habits and ways of life. They mortgaged their lands—all that was left to them—with great coolness and a superstitious faith in the future—Virginians are prone to hanker after mortgages—and spent the money untroubled by any reflections where any more was to come from when that was gone.

They were intense pleasure lovers. In that happy afternoon haze in which they had lived until the storm broke, pleasure was the chief end of man. So now, the whole county turned out to see two or three broken-down hacks, and a green colt or two, race for the mythical stakes. It is true, a green silk bag, embroidered in gold, with the legend "$300" hung aloft on a tall pole, for the sweepstakes, but it did not contain three hundred dollars, but about one-half of it in gold, and a check drawn by the president of the Jockey Club against the treasurer for the balance. Most of the members had not paid their dues, and the treasurer didn't know where the money was to come from, nor the president either, for that matter; but it takes a good deal to discount a Virginian's faith in the future. The public, too, was fully acquainted with the state of affairs, and the fact that there was any gold at all in the bag, would eventually be in the nature of a pleasant surprise.

The people, in carriages, or on horseback, bore little resemblance to the usual country gathering. They were gentlepeople tinged with rusticity. All of them had good, high sounding Anglo-Saxon names. There was some magnificence of an antique pattern. One huge family ark was drawn by four sleek old horses, with a venerable black coachman on the box, and inside a superb old lady with a black veil falling over her white hair. There were but two really correct equipages in the field. One was a trim, chocolate-colored victoria, with brown horses and a chocolate-colored coachman to match. In it sat a showy woman, with a profusion of dazzling blonde hair, and beside her was an immaculately well dressed blonde man. The turnout looked like a finely finished photograph among a lot of dingy old family portraits.

The other carriage that would have passed muster was a large and handsome landau, respectfully called "the Isleham carriage," and in it sat Colonel Berkeley and his daughter Olivia. The Colonel was a genuine Virginia colonel, and claimed to be the last man in the State to wear a ruffled shirt bosom. A billowy expanse of thread cambric ruffles rushed out of his waistcoat; his snow white hair was carefully combed down upon his coat collar. At the carriage door stood his double—an elderly negro as grizzled as his master, to whom he bore that curious resemblance that comes of fifty years association. This resemblance was very much increased when Colonel Berkeley's back was turned, and in the privacy of the kitchen, Petrarch—or more commonly Pete—pished and pshawed and railed and swore in the colonel's most inimitable manner. Each, too, possessed a type of aggressive piety, which in Colonel Berkeley took the form of a loud declaration that a gentleman, in order to be a gentleman, must be a member of the Episcopal Church. This once accomplished, the Colonel was willing to allow liberally for the weaknesses of human nature, and considered too great strictness of behavior as "deuced ungentlemanlike, begad." Petrarch regarded himself as a second Isaiah the prophet, and a vessel of election—having reached the stage of perfectibility—a usual thing in the experience of a genuine African. The Colonel described Petrarch as "that infernal rascally boy of mine," and this "boy" was the one individual he had never been able to overawe or silence. Possibly an exception might be made to this in Miss Olivia, who sitting up, slim and straight and pretty, was treated by her father with elaborate old-fashioned courtesy. Colonel Berkeley was in a particularly happy and virtuous frame of mind on this day. This was his first appearance in public since his return from Europe, where a serious bodily injury had kept him during the whole four years of the war. He gloried in the consciousness that he was no renegade, but had returned to the sacred soil as soon as he possibly could, when he might have been enjoying himself elsewhere. When the Colonel said "the State of Virginia," he really meant the whole planetary system. Nevertheless, two weeks in his beloved Virginia had bored him dreadfully, and he was "more orkarder," as

Petrarch expressed it, than any other two weeks of his whole life. The Campdown races he hailed as a godsend. He had a good competence left, in spite of having sent orders to his agents to convert lands, stocks, bonds, and everything, into Confederate securities—cotton bonds, Confederate gunboat stock, anything in which the State of Virginia was bound up. As far as in him lay, he had made ducks and drakes of a splendid fortune, from the finest and most disinterested motives that ever inspired a mistaken old gentleman, but fate had befriended him against his will. An investment at the North that the colonel had vainly tried to throw in the general wreck, had escaped confiscation, and had increased, a hundredfold in value. His orders to sell half of Isleham, his family place, for Confederate money, had arrived too late for his agent to carry it out. He had done the handsome thing, as it was esteemed, and after having practiced the strictest virtue, he was rewarded with all the pleasures that are commonly supposed to be the reward of vice.

"Don't you think, papa," the young girl said to him at once, "that we should go up on the grand stand? It might look a little—a little standoffish for us to remain here—and the county people—"

The Virginians inherit from their English ancestry, a vast and preposterous respect for their county people—and Miss Olivia Berkeley, fresh from Paris and London, was more anxious that no fault should be found with her by these out-of-the-way provincials than any of the fine people she had met during a considerable transatlantic experience. So was Colonel Berkeley—but there was a fly in his ointment.

"I would with pleasure, my love, but damme if those Hibbses are not sitting up on the stand along with their betters—and I won't rub elbows with the Hibbses. It's everywhere the same. Society is so infernally mixed now that I am always expecting to meet my tailor at dinner. I thought certainly, in old Virginia, the people would know how to keep the canaille in their places, and there, by George, sits a family like the Hibbses staring me in the face."

"Yes," replied Olivia, smiling. "It's everywhere the same—you are bound to meet some of the Hibbses everywhere in the world—so we might as well do the right thing in spite of them. Petrarch, open the carriage door."

The Colonel, with old-fashioned gallantry, assisted his daughter to alight, and giving her his arm, they crossed the track in full view of the grand stand, and went up the rickety wooden stairs at the end.

At no period in her life had Olivia Berkeley felt herself so thoroughly on exhibition as then. Her figure, her air—both of which were singularly graceful and refined—her gown which was Paris-made—all were minutely examined by hundreds of eyes that had not seen her since, as a pretty, half-grown girl, she went to church and paid visits under the charge of a demure governess. After they had crossed the white track, they were greeted by numerous gentlemen who sauntered back and forth about the quarter-stretch. Colonel Berkeley was elaborately gracious, and Olivia was by nature affable—to all except the Hibbses. But when they passed that inoffending family, the Colonel stalked on pointedly oblivious, and Olivia's slight bow was not warming or cheering.

People moved up to shake hands with them—girls of Olivia's age, soft voiced, matronly women, elderly men, a little shaky and broken, as all the old men looked after the war—and young men with something of the camp hanging to them still. Olivia was all grace, kindness, and tact. She had forgotten nobody.

Meanwhile Petrarch, who had followed them, managed to edge up to her and whisper:

"Miss 'Livy, ain't dat ar Marse French Pembroke an' he b'rer Miles? Look a-yander by de aige o' de bench."

Olivia glanced that way, and a slight wave of color swept over her face—and at that moment "Marse French's b'rer Miles" turned his full face toward her.

He was a mere lad, of eighteen at the utmost. One side of his face, as she had first seen his profile, was of the purest Greek beauty. But on the other side, a shot had done dreadful work. One eye was drawn out of place. A horrid gash in the cheek remained, and one side of the mouth was painfully disfigured. On the same side, an arm was missing.

A torrent of pity almost overwhelmed Olivia as she looked at the boy—her little playmate in years gone by. And then the elder brother caught her eye, and bowed and smiled. He did not possess the beauty that had once belonged to Miles. He was dark and tanned, and his features had a manly irregularity. But he stood up straight and tall, and had the figure of a soldier. In a moment or two Olivia was shaking hands with Miles, looking straight and boldly into his face, as if there was nothing remarkable there. But just as she touched French Pembroke's hand, the blonde woman in the victoria came within her line of vision.

Olivia threw up her head, and greeted Pembroke with a kind of chilling sweetness. But this all dissolved toward Miles.

"How delightful to see you again," she said. "I suppose I shall have to say Mr. Miles now, although I never can think of you as anything but a dear little tormenting boy."

The ghost of a smile—his smile was a mere contortion—came into Miles' face—and while he talked, he thrust his one hand into his trousers pocket with a gesture of boyish shyness. Olivia thought she heard the tell-tale rattle of marbles in the pocket.

"I've—I've been a soldier since I saw you," he said, with a boy's mixture of pride and diffidence.

"So I hear," answered Olivia, with a pretty air of severity, "ran away from school, I believe."

"Yes," said Miles, his diffidence disappearing before his pride. "I was big enough to carry a musket. Though I wasn't but sixteen, I was taller than the captain of my company. Soldiering was fun until—until—." He began to blush furiously, but kept on after a moment. "I didn't mind sleeping in the mud, or anything. A man oughtn't to mind that sort of thing, Olivia—if you'll let me call you Olivia."

"Of course I will," replied Olivia gayly. "Do you think I want to appear any older than I am?" Then she turned to Pembroke and said, "I was sorry not to have seen you the day you came to Isleham. We met last in Paris."

"I hope to see as much of Isleham as we did in the old days," answered Pembroke. His voice was rather remarkable, it was so clear and well modulated.

"I hope," began Miles, stammering a little, "that—that you and the Colonel understood my not—why I didn't come to see you in Paris."

"Not fully," answered Olivia, pleasantly. "You must come over to Isleham and explain it—if you can. Have you seen papa yet?"

"I see him now," said Pembroke with a smile, "shaking hands with Mrs. Peyton."

Olivia smiled too. There had been a flirtation between Mrs. Peyton and Colonel Berkeley forty odd years before, and as everything that happened in the community was perfectly well known by everybody else, the episode had crystallized into a tradition. Colonel Berkeley had been known to swear that Sally Peyton in her youth was a jilt. Mrs. Peyton always said that Tom Berkeley was not to be depended on. The Colonel was saying to Mrs. Peyton in his grandest tones:

"Madam, Time has passed you by."

"Ah, my dear Colonel," responded Mrs. Peyton with a quizzical look at Colonel Berkeley's elaborate toilet and flamboyant shirt ruffles, "we can't cross the dead line of sixty without showing it. Even art cannot conceal it."

"Just like Sally Peyton's sharp tongue," the colonel growled sotto voce—while a suppressed guffaw from Pete on the verge of the group, showed the remark was not lost on that factotum.

"And Petrarch too," cried Mrs. Peyton in her fine, jovial old voice, holding out her hand.

Pete shuffled up and took her hand in his black paw.

"Howdy, Miss Sally. Lordy, marster done tole de truf—you looks jes ez young an' chipper—How's Mandy?"

"Mandy has lost her senses since old Abe Lincoln made you all free. She's left me and gone to Richmond to go to school—the old idiot."

"Hi! I allers did like Mandy, but I ain't got no use fer dem niggers dat kin read 'n write. Readin' an' writin' is fer white folks."

"Shut up, you black rascal," roared the Colonel, nevertheless highly delighted. "Madam, may I present my daughter—Olivia, my child."

Olivia came up, and Mrs. Peyton kissed her affectionately, but not before a rapid glance which took in all there was of her.

"Like her sainted mother," began the Colonel, dramatically.

"Not a bit," briskly answered Mrs. Peyton. "A Berkeley all over, if ever I saw one. Child, I hope you are as nice as you are pretty."

"Nobody ever told me I wasn't nice," responded Olivia with a smile.

"And not spoiled by your foreign travels?"

"Not in the least."

Clang! Clang! Clang! goes the saddling bell.

"What do you think?" says Olivia laughing. "Papa has entered Dashaway. You know he is twelve years old, and as Petrarch says, he hasn't any wind left—but papa wouldn't listen to anybody."

"Yes, that's Tom Berkeley all over. Ah, my dear, I could tell you something that happened forty-two years ago, in which I promise you, I got the better of your father."

The horses by this time are coming out. They are an ordinary looking lot except one spanking roan, the property of the despised Hibbses, and Dashaway, a gray thoroughbred, a good deal like Colonel Berkeley himself, but like him, with certain physical defects. The gray has a terrific wheeze, and the hair on his fetlocks is perfectly white. But he holds his head up gallantly, and gives a tremendous snort which nearly shakes the mite of a darkey off his back. All the jockeys are negro boys. There is no pool-selling, but the gentlemen make bets among themselves and with the ladies. The transactions if small, are exciting.

Colonel Berkeley's presence hardly prevents a laugh as the gray ambles past the grand stand, snorting and blowing like a porpoise. The Colonel, however, has unshaken confidence in Dashaway. Is he not of the best blood of Sir Henry, and didn't he win fourteen hundred dollars for the Colonel on the Campdown course the year before the war? Colonel Berkeley knows a horse well enough—but to know horses and to know one's own horse are two things.

Colonel Berkeley, leaning over the fence, is giving his directions, in a loud voice, to the little darkey, who is nearly ashy with fright. He knows what is expected of him, and he knows Dashaway's deficiencies.

"Now, sir, you are to make the running from the half-mile post. Keep well up with the horse in the lead, but don't attempt to pass him until you have turned the half-mile."

"Yes, sah," answers the small jockey, trembling. "But Dashaway, he c'yarn run much, sah, 'thout blowin', an'—an'—"

"Zounds, sirrah, do you mean to instruct me about my own horse? Now listen you young imp. Use the whip moderately, Dashaway comes of stock that won't stand whip and spur. If he runs away, just give him his head, and if you don't remember every word I tell you, by the Lord Harry, I'll make you dance by the time you are out of the saddle!"

"Good Gord A'mighty, marster," puts in Petrarch. "Dashaway, he ain' never gwi' run away. He too ole, an' he ain't strong 'nuff—"

"Good Gad, sir, was ever a man so tormented by such a set of black rascals? Hold your tongue—don't let me hear another word from you, not another word, sir."

The jockey, who takes the Colonel's words at their full value, which Petrarch discounts liberally, begins to stutter with fright.

"M—m—marster, ef I jes' kin git Dashaway 'long wid de res'—"

"Silence, sir," shouts the Colonel, "and remember every word I tell you, or——" Colonel Berkeley's appalling countenance and uplifted cane complete the rest.

Dashaway is not only conspicuously the worst of the lot, but the most troublesome. Half a dozen good starts might be made but for Dashaway. At last the flag drops. "Go!" yells the starter, and the horses are off. Dashaway takes his place promptly in the rear, and daylight steadily widens between him and the last horse. As the field comes thundering down the homestretch the spanking roan well in the lead, Dashaway is at least a quarter of a mile behind, blowing like a whale, and the jockey is whipping furiously, his arm flying around like a windmill. The Colonel is fairly dancing with rage.

Colonel Berkeley is not the man to lose a race to the Hibbses with composure, and Petrarch's condolences, reminiscences, prophecies and deductions were not of a consolatory character.

"Ole Marse, I done tole you, Dashaway warn't fitten ter run, at de very startment. He been a mighty good horse, but he c'yarn snuffle de battle fum befo', an' say Hay! hay! like de horse in de Bible no mo'."

"Shut up, sir—shut up. Religion and horse racing don't mix," roars the Colonel.

"Naw suh, dey doan! When de horse racin' folks is burnin' in de lake full er brimstone an' sulphur, de 'ligious folks will be rastlin' wid de golden harps—" Petrarch's sermon is cut ruthlessly short by Colonel Berkeley suddenly catching sight of the unfortunate jockey in a vain attempt to get out of the way. But his day of reckoning had come. Petrarch had collared him, and the Colonel proceeded to give him what he called a dressing-down, liberally punctuated with flourishes of a bamboo cane.

"Didn't I tell you," he was shouting to the unhappy youngster, "to make the running—*to make the running, hay?*"

"M—m—marster, I 'clar to Gord, I thot' Dashaway wuz gw'in' to drap 'fo I git him to de half-mile pos'—"

"*Drap*—you scoundrel, *drap*! The blood of Sir Henry *drap*! You confounded rascal, you pulled that horse," etc., etc., etc.

Mrs. Peyton laughed. "It does my heart good to hear Tom Berkeley raging like that. It reminds me that we are not all dead or changed, as it seems to me sometimes. Your father and I have had passages-at-arms in *my* time, I can tell you, Olivia."

Clang! presently again. It is the saddling bell once more. But there is no Dashaway in this race. Nevertheless it is very exciting. There are half a dozen horses, and after the start is made it looks to be anybody's race. Even as they come pounding down the straight sweep of the last two furlongs, it would be hard to pick out the probable winner. The people on the grand stand have gone wild—they are shouting names, the men waving their hats, the women standing up on benches to see as two or three horses gradually draw away from the others, and a desperate struggle is promised within the last thirty lengths. And just at this moment, when everybody's attention is fixed on the incoming horses, French Pembroke has slipped across the track and is speaking to the blonde woman in the victoria. His face does not look pleasant. He has chosen this moment, when all attention is fixed on something else to speak to her, so that it will not be observed—and although he adopts the subterfuge, he despises it. Nor does the blonde woman fail to see through it. She does not relish being spoken to on the sly as it were. Nothing, however, disturbs the cheerful urbanity of the gentleman by her side. He gets out of the carriage and grasps Pembroke by the hand. He calls him "mon cher" a vulgar mode of address which Pembroke resents with a curt "Good-morning, Mr. Ahlberg," and then he lifts his hat to the lady whom he calls Madame Koller. "Why did you not come before?" she asks, "you might have known it would be dull enough."

"Don't you know everybody here?"

"Oh, yes," replied Madame Koller, sighing profoundly. "I remember all of them—and most of the men have called. Some of them are so strange. They stay all day when they come. And such queer carriages."

"And the costumes. The costumes!" adds Mr. Ahlberg on the ground.

Pembroke felt a sense of helpless indignation. He answered Mr. Ahlberg by turning his back, and completely ignoring that excessively stylish person.

"You must remember the four years' harrowing they have been through," he says to Madame Koller. "But they are so thoroughly established in their own esteem," he adds with a little malice, "that they are indifferent even to the disapproval of Madame Koller. I am glad to see you looking so well. I must, however, leave you now, as I am one of the managers, and must look after the weighing."

"Now you are going away because I have been disagreeable," remarked Madame Koller reproachfully. "And poor Ahlberg—"

"Must take care of you, and do his best to amuse you," answered Pembroke with a laugh and a look that classed Ahlberg with Madame's poodle or her parrot. "Good-bye," and in a minute he was gone. Madame Koller looked sulky. Mr. Ahlberg's good humor and composure were perfectly unruffled.

Hardly any one noticed Pembroke's little expedition except Mrs. Peyton and Olivia Berkeley. Mrs. Peyton mounted a pair of large gold spectacles, and then remarked to Olivia:

"My dear, there's French Pembroke talking to my niece, Eliza Peyton—" Mrs. Peyton was a Peyton before she married one—"Madame Elise Koller she now calls herself."

"Yes, I see."

"I suppose you saw a good deal of her in Paris, and my sister-in-law, Sarah Scaife that was—now Madame Schmidt. She showed me the dear departed's picture the other day—a horrid little wretch he looked, while my brother, Edmund Peyton, was the handsomest young man in the county."

"We saw Madame Koller quite often," said Olivia. Mrs. Peyton was amazingly clever as a mind reader, and saw in a moment there was no love lost between Olivia Berkeley and Madame Koller.

"And that Mr. Ahlberg. Sarah Scaife says he is a cousin of Eliza's—I mean Elise's—husband."

"I should think if anybody knew the facts in the case it would be Sarah Scaife, as you call her," replied Olivia laughing. "I believe he is a very harmless kind of a man."

At that Mrs. Peyton took off her spectacles and looked at Olivia keenly.

"I hate to believe you are a goose," she said, good-naturedly; "but you must be very innocent. Harmless! That is the very thing that man is not."

"So papa says, but I think it comes from Mr. Ahlberg eating asparagus with his fingers and not knowing how to play whist, or something of the kind. I have seen him on and off at watering places, and in Paris for two or three years. I never saw him do anything that wasn't quite right—and I never heard anything against him except what you and papa say—and that is rather indefinite."

"And you didn't observe my niece with French Pembroke, did you?"

Olivia Berkeley's face turned a warm color. Such very plain spoken persons as Mrs. Peyton were a little embarrassing. But just then came the sound of the Colonel's voice, raised at a considerable distance.

"Olivia, my love—God bless my soul—Mrs. Peyton—there's that charming niece of yours—what a creature she was when she lived in this county as Eliza Peyton—a regular stunner, begad—I must go and speak to her—and my particular friend, Ahlberg—excuse me a moment, my love." Colonel Berkeley stalked across the track, receiving all the attention which Pembroke had tried to avoid. Life in his beloved Virginia had almost driven the Colonel distracted by its dullness, and he could not but welcome a fellow creature from the outside. He buttoned his light overcoat trimly around his still handsome figure, and bowed majestically when he reached the carriage. Madame Koller returned the bow with a brilliant smile. She was beginning to feel very much alone, albeit she was in her native county, and she welcomed Colonel Berkeley as a deliverer. Evidently she soothed him about Dashaway. Pembroke, passing by, heard scraps like the following:

"I have seen just such things at the Grand Prix—"

"Madame, the infernal system here of putting up irresponsible negro boys—"

"I could see he had a superb stride—"

"Dashaway, Madame Koller, comes from the very best stock in the State of Virginia."

The day wore on, and by dint of spinning things out most unconscionably it was dusk of the clear autumn evening before the cavalcade took the dusty white road toward home. In "the Isleham carriage" Colonel Berkeley leaned back and waxed confidential with his daughter.

"My dear, Eliza Peyton—Madame Koller I should say—is what you young sprigs call green—excessively green. She imagines because I am old I am a fool. And that precious scamp, Ahlberg—"

"Why do you call him a scamp, papa?"

"Why do I call Petrarch an African?"

"Mrs. Peyton seems to have some kind of a prejudice to Mr. Ahlberg, too."

"Aha, trust Sally Peyton to see for herself. She's devilish tricky, is Sally Peyton—not that I have any cause to complain of it—none whatever. She's very sharp. But we'll go and call some day on Eli—Madame Koller. She's not bad company for the country—and I've heard she could sing, too."

"Yes, we will go," answered Olivia, suppressing a yawn. "It's in the country, as you say."

CHAPTER II.

DOES anybody ever ask what becomes of the *prime donne* who break down early? Madame Koller could have told something about their miseries, from the first struggling steps up to the pinnacle when they can fight with managers, down again to the point when the most dreadful sound that nature holds—so she thought—a hiss—laid them figuratively among the dead. Nature generally works methodically, but in Madame Koller's case, she seemed to take a delight in producing grapes from thorns. Without one atom of artistic heredity, surroundings or atmosphere to draw upon, Eliza Peyton had come into the world an artist. She had a voice, and she grew up with the conviction that there was nothing in the world but voices and pianos. It is not necessary to repeat how in her girlhood, by dint of her widowed mother marrying a third rate German professor, she got to Munich and to Milan—nor how the voice, at first astonishingly pure and beautiful, suddenly lost its pitch, then disappeared altogether. It is true that after a time it came back to her partially. She could count on it for an hour at a time, but no more. Of course there was no longer any career for her, and she nearly went crazy with grief—then she consoled herself with M. Koller, an elderly Swiss manufacturer. In some way, although she was young and handsome and accomplished, she found in her continental travels that the best Americans and English avoided the Kollers. This she rashly attributed to the fact of her having had a brief professional career, and she became as anxious to conceal it as she had once been anxious to pursue it. M. Koller was a hypochondriac, and went from Carlsbad to Wiesbaden, from Wiesbaden to Hyéres, from Hyéres to Aix-les-Bains. He was always fancying himself dying, but one day at Vichy, death came quite unceremoniously and claimed him just as he had made up his mind to get well. Thus Eliza Koller found herself a widow, still young and handsome, with a comfortable fortune, and a negative mother to play propriety. She went straight to Paris as soon as the period of her mourning was over. It was then toward the latter part of the civil war in America, and there were plenty of Southerners in Paris. There she met Colonel Berkeley and Olivia, and for the first time in her adult life, she had a fixed place in society—there was a circle in which she was known.

What most troubled her, was what rôle to take up—whether she should be an American, a French woman, an Italian, a German, or a cosmopolitan. For she was like all, and was distinctively none. In Paris at that time, she met a cousin of her late husband—Mr. Ahlberg, also a Swiss, but in the Russian diplomatic service. He was a sixth Secretary of Legation, and had hard work making his small salary meet his expenses. He was a handsome man, very blonde, and extremely well-dressed. Madame Koller often wondered if his tailor were not a very confiding person. For Ahlberg's part, he sincerely liked his cousin, as he called her, and quite naturally slipped into the position of a friend of the family. Everything perhaps would have been arranged to his satisfaction, if just at that time the war had not closed, and French Pembroke and his brother came to Paris that the surgeons might work upon poor Miles. They could not but meet often at the Berkeleys, and Pembroke, it must be admitted, was not devoid of admiration for the handsome Madame Koller, who had the divine voice—when she could be persuaded to sing, which was not often. He had been rather attentive to her, much to Ahlberg's disgust. And to Ahlberg's infinite rage, Madame Koller fell distinctly and unmistakably in love with Pembroke. If Ahlberg had only known the truth, Pembroke was really the first gentleman that poor Madame Koller had ever known intimately since her childhood in Virginia. Certainly the wildest stretch of imagination could not call the late Koller a gentleman, and even Ahlberg himself, although a member of the diplomatic corps, hardly came under that description.

Pembroke had a kind of hazy idea that widows could take care of themselves. Besides, he was not really in love with her—only a little dazzled by her voice and her yellow hair. His wrath may be imagined when after a considerable wrench in tearing himself away from Paris, and when he had begun to regard Olivia Berkeley with that lofty approval which sometimes precedes love making, to return to Virginia, and in six weeks to find Madame Schmidt and Madame Koller established at their old place, The Beeches, and Ahlberg, who had been their shadow for two years, living at the village tavern. He felt that this following him, on the part of Madame Koller, made him ridiculous. He was mortally afraid of being laughed at about it. Instead of holding his own stoutly in acrid discussions with Colonel Berkeley, Pembroke began to be afraid of the old gentleman's pointed allusions to the widow. He even got angry with poor little Miles when the boy ventured upon a little sly chaff. As for Olivia Berkeley, she took Madame Koller's conduct in coming to Virginia in high dudgeon, with that charming inconsequence of noble and inexperienced women. What particular offense it gave her, beyond the appearance of following Pembroke, which was shocking to her good taste, she could not have explained to have saved her life. But with Madame Koller she took a tone of politeness, sweet yet chilly, like frozen cream—and the same in a less degree, toward Pembroke. She seemed to say, "Odious and underbred as this thing is, I, you see, can afford to be magnanimous." Colonel Berkeley chuckled at this on the part of his daughter, as he habitually did at the innocent foibles of his fellow creatures. It was very innocent, very feminine, and very exasperating.

Nevertheless, within a week the big landau was drawn up, and Colonel Berkeley and his daughter set forth, *en grand tenue*, with Petrarch on the box, to call on Madame Koller. The Colonel had never ceased teasing his daughter to go. Time hung heavy on his hands, and although he had not found Madame Koller particularly captivating elsewhere, and Madame Schmidt bored him to death upon the few occasions when she appeared, yet, when he was at Isleham, the ladies at The Beeches assumed quite a fascinating aspect to his imagination. The Colonel had a private notion of his own that Madame Koller had been a little too free with her income, and that a year's retirement would contribute to the health of her finances. Olivia, however, believed that Madame Koller had but one object in returning to America, and that was because Pembroke had come. She remembered one evening in Paris, Pembroke had "dropped in," American fashion. The doctors had then said that nothing could be done to restore poor Miles to comeliness—and meanwhile, another blow had fallen upon the two brothers. Their only sister, Elizabeth, a handsome, high spirited girl, older than they, had died—and there had been a violent breach between her and their father to which death alone put a truce. When the country was overrun with troops, a Federal officer had protected the plantation as far as he could, had saved the old father from the consequences of his own rash conduct, and had taken a deep and tender interest in the daughter. This was enough to blast Elizabeth's life. She gave up her lover—silently, but with a strange unyielding gentleness, she kept aloof from her father. She was not condemned to suffer long. The unhappy father followed her swiftly to the old burying ground at Malvern. Men commonly seek distraction in griefs. Pembroke was like the rest. He was popular, especially among the English colony where his love of sports and manly accomplishments made him a favorite—to say nothing of that prestige, which attaches to a man who has seen service. He had gone into the war a lieutenant, and had come out as major of his ragged, half-starved regiment. Therefore when Pembroke idled and amused himself in Paris, for some time Olivia could only feel sympathy for him. She knew well enough that his means were small and the company he kept was liable to diminish them—but after a while, she began to feel a hot indignation against him. So on this particular evening, the Colonel falling asleep opportunely, she took occasion to express her opinion to Pembroke, that their ruined country needed the presence and the service of every man she could call her own. Pembroke defended himself warmly at first. He came for Miles' sake—the boy whom he had thought safe at school, and who ran away in the very last days of the war to enlist—and almost the last shot that was fired—so Pembroke said bitterly—disfigured the boy as he now was. Miles had been eager to come, although Pembroke was convinced from the beginning that neither the French, nor any other surgeons could repair the work of that shot. He admitted that the boy had borne the final decision with great manliness and courage "for such a little chap," the elder brother said fondly. When pressed hard by Olivia about returning home, Pembroke though had no resource but epigrams.

"At all events," she said presently, with a pretty air of heroism, "Papa and I are going home just as soon as papa can do without his crutch. Papa is a patriot, although he does talk so remarkably sometimes."

"Then, after you have got back, you can let me know how you like Virginia as it is, and perhaps I will follow," he answered, laughing in a very exasperating way, Olivia thought. But when the Berkeleys got home they found that the Pembrokes had arrived some weeks before them—and soon afterward Madame Koller and her mother turned up quite unexpectedly at their deserted old place, only to be followed shortly after by Ahlberg, who, from his abode at the village tavern rode over every day on a sorry nag, to see Madame Koller.

Imagine all this in a provincial country neighborhood!

Mr. Cole, the clergyman of Petsworth parish, was a bachelor, a small, neatly-featured person, suspected of High Church leanings. The Colonel had bluntly inquired of him if he intended to call on Madame Koller.

"Hardly, I think, sir," responded Mr. Cole, with much severity. "She has not once been to church since she returned to the county—and she only two miles off—and I hear that she and her friend Mr. Ahlberg play billiards all day long Sunday, when they are not playing cards."

"Only the more reason for you to convert the heathen, ha! ha!" answered the Colonel—"and let me tell you, Cole, if you hadn't been a clergyman, you would have been a regular slayer among the women—and the heathen in this case is about as pretty a heathen as you can find in the State of Virginia, sir."

Evidently these remarks made a great impression on Mr. Cole, for on the sunny afternoon, when Colonel Berkeley and Olivia drove up to the door of The Beeches, they saw a clerical looking figure disappear ahead of them within the doorway.

"The parson's here, by Jove," chuckled the Colonel.

The house was modern and rather showy. Inside there were evidences that Madame Koller was not devoid of taste or money either. The Berkeleys were ushered into a big square drawing-room, where, seated in a high-backed chair, with his feet barely touching the floor, was the little clergyman.

"Why, Cole, I am deuced glad you took my advice," cried the Colonel, advancing with outstretched hand and with a kind of hearty good fellowship that pleased Mr. Cole, and yet frightened him a little. He was a good soul and divided his small salary with his mother, but he thought Colonel Berkeley's society rather dangerous for a clergyman. He used too many expletives, and was altogether too free in his notions of what a churchman should be—for the Colonel was a stanch churchman, and would have sworn like a pirate at anybody who questioned his orthodoxy.

"Doing missionary work, hay, Mr. Cole?" continued Colonel Berkeley, while Olivia and Mr. Cole shook hands.

A faint pink mounted into the clergyman's face. His curiosity had got the better of him, but the excellent little man fancied it was his Christian charity that won the victory.

"Well, Colonel," he begun, "upon reflection I concluded it was my duty to call on Madame Koller. I wasn't in this parish—in fact, I wasn't ordained at the time Madame Koller was Miss Eliza Peyton, and Madame Schmidt was Mrs. Edward Peyton. And being the niece of my excellent friend—Mrs. Sally Peyton—"

"Excellent friend, eh—well, don't you trust Sally Peyton too far, my good fellow. She was a mighty uncertain kind of a friend thirty or forty years ago—not that I have any particular reason for saying so. But you are quite right in paying your respects to Eliza Peyton—I mean Madame Koller, and I only hope she'll find our society agreeable enough to stay here."

A considerable wait ensued. Olivia had begun to wonder how long it took Madame Koller to make a complete toilet, when a white hand moved the curtain from a doorway, and noiselessly and gently Madame Koller entered.

She was heartily glad to see them—their call was not very prompt, but it would have been a cruel mortification had they omitted to come. Olivia's hand she pressed—so she did the Colonel's—and also Mr. Cole's, who colored quite violently, although he struggled for self-possession.

"We are very glad you have come," said Olivia, with her sweetest affability, "you will be a great acquisition to the neighborhood. You see, I am already beginning to think more of our own neighborhood than all the rest of the universe."

"Thank you for your kindness," answered Madame Koller, with equal cordiality. The two women, however, did not cease to examine each other like gladiators.

"And Mr. Cole, I think you were not here when I lived at The Beeches as a girl."

"No, madam," replied Mr. Cole, who had now shaded from a red to a pink.

"And did I not have the pleasure of seeing you at the Campdown races the other day?"

Mr. Cole turned pale and nearly dropped off his chair. The Colonel roared out his pleasant cheery laugh.

"No madam, you did not." Mr. Cole made his denial so emphatic that he was ashamed of himself for it afterwards.

"But you, Miss Berkeley, were there. My cousin Ahlberg saw you. He praised you. He complimented you. 'I have often seen that face,' he said. 'There are some faces which one remembers even in the whirl of the greatest cities. I drive around the Bois de Boulogne—once—twice—three times. I speak to a hundred friends. I see a thousand faces. They pass before me like shadows of the night. One face strikes me. It rises like a star from out the sea. Ah, I exclaim, 'here is another photograph for my mental portrait gallery.'"

Neither the Colonel nor Olivia was fully prepared to accept Ahlberg. Consequently, Madame Koller's remark was received with a cool smile by Olivia—and a sniff by the Colonel. But Mr. Cole was quite carried away by Madame Koller's declamatory manner, and her really beautiful voice.

"What a gift of tongues," he said. "Madame Koller, if a—er—public speaker—a religious instructor had your felicity of expression—"

"I trust," answered Madame, "some time to have the pleasure of hearing *your* felicity of expression. I am not what you call a Christian. I believe in a system of ultimate good—a philosophy if you will—"

"Yes, yes," cordially chimed in Colonel Berkeley with something dangerously like a wink, "I knew Madame, as soon as I saw you that you believed in a system. It's very useful and elastic and philosophic."

Madame playfully waved her hand at the colonel, and turned to Mr. Cole.

"We will be friends, nevertheless," she said with a captivating smile. "I will visit your church in the morning, and you will return to luncheon with me, and we will have a little game of billiards afterward."

Mr. Cole's delicate face grew ashy. He, John Chrysostom Cole, playing billiards on Sunday! What would his mother say—and what would the bishop say! Olivia looked a little shocked because of course Madame Koller must know better. Not so the Colonel. He laughed heartlessly at Mr. Cole, and began to think Eliza Peyton was a more amusing person than he had fancied.

"Madame Koller," began Mr. Cole solemnly after a moment, "your long absence from this country—your unfamiliarity with clergymen perhaps—and with the American Sabbath—"

"Oh, yes, I remember the American Sabbath very well," replied Madame Koller laughing and raising her eyebrows. "My aunt, Mrs. Peyton, always took me to church with her, and I had to listen to Dr. Steptoe's sermons. Oh those sermons! However," she added, turning her expressive eyes full on Mr. Cole. "I know, I *know* yours must be very different. Well, I will go. And forgive me, if I sometimes shock you—forgive and pity me."

Mr. Cole thought that only a heart of stone could have hardened against that pretty appeal. And the widow was so deliciously charming with her half-foreign manner and her whole-foreign look. But billiards on Sunday!

"Extend the invitation to me, ma'am," said the Colonel. "I go to church on Sunday—I have no system, just the plain religious belief of a churchman and a gentleman—my ancestors were not a lot of psalm-singing hypocrites, but cavaliers, madam, from the Court of Charles the Second. But after I've been to church to please my conscience and my daughter, I don't mind pleasing myself a little. I'll play billiards with you—"

The door opened and Ahlberg appeared. Now Mr. Ahlberg was not a favorite of Colonel Berkeley's at any time—still less of Olivia's; but it was in the country, and it was very, very dull, so he got the most cordial greeting he had ever had from either of them. The conversation became general, and as soon as Ahlberg had the opportunity, he edged toward Olivia. He was no gentle, unsophisticated creature, like Mr. Cole. He knew that Olivia Berkeley's polite and self-possessed manner toward him concealed a certain hardness. He made no particular headway in her good graces he saw—and not much more in the Colonel's. But both gentlemen were hard up for amusement, and each was willing to be amused, so, when Mr. Ahlberg, after a few well-bred vacuities with Olivia, devoted himself to Colonel Berkeley, he was rewarded with the intimation that the Colonel would call on him at the village tavern, and this was followed up by another hint of a dinner invitation to follow. This cheered Mr. Ahlberg very much, for to tell the truth he was as near starvation as a man could be in this nineteenth century, who had money in his pocket. If, however, Mr. Ahlberg had made it his business to horrify Mr. Cole, he could not have done it more thoroughly. He bewailed the absence of book-makers at the races, and wished to know why elections were not held in America on Sunday, took occasion to say that religion was merely an affair of the State, and he too was a believer in a system. When they all rose to go, poor Mr. Cole was quite limp and overcome, but he made an effort to retain his self-possession. He urged both Madame Koller and Mr. Ahlberg to attend the morning service on the following Sunday. Both promised conditionally.

The clergyman had walked over from the rectory where his mother presided over his modest establishment.

"Come, Cole," cried the Colonel, who was the soul of hospitality, "here's another seat in the carriage. Come back to dinner with us. I've got some capital champagne, and Olivia will play for you."

"I don't care about the champagne, thank you," answered Mr. Cole, "but I'll come for the pleasure of Miss Olivia's playing and her society also."

Scarcely had the carriage turned into the lane, when Mr. Cole burst forth:

"Miss Olivia, did you ever meet a more godless person in your life than Mr. Ahlberg?"

"I don't think I ever did," answered Olivia, with much sincerity.

"But the widow—Eliza Peyton—eh, Cole? I think you have made some headway there," cried the Colonel, wagging his head at the little clergyman. Mr. Cole's heart began to thump. Strange it was that although he ought, as a Christian and a clergyman, to disapprove of Madame Koller with her beautiful blonde hair, he could not find it in his heart to feel it. Nevertheless he could say it easily enough.

"I very much doubt, sir, the propriety of my visiting at The Beeches."

"Pooh, pooh. You'll get over it," chuckled Colonel Berkeley.

Ah, John Chrysostom! Has it never been known that the outward man denounced what the inward man yearned and hankered after? At this very moment do you not remember the turn of Madame Koller's handsome head, and the faint perfume that exhaled from her trailing gown?

"We must invite them to dinner," said the Colonel, decidedly. "Cole, you must come, too. That poor devil, Ahlberg, is almost starved at the tavern on fried chicken three times a day, and claret from the tavern bar."

CHAPTER III.

A ROUND of solemn afternoon dinings followed the return of the Berkeleys to Isleham, and were scrupulously returned. But both the Colonel and Olivia felt that it would not be well to include any of the county gentry the day Madame Koller and Mr. Ahlberg were to dine with them. Mr. Cole had already been invited—and Colonel Berkeley of his own free will, without saying a word to Olivia, asked the two Pembrokes. Olivia, when she heard of this, was intensely vexed. She had used both sarcasm and persuasion on Pembroke in Paris to get him home, and he had laughed at her. Yet she was firmly convinced, as soon as Madame Koller expressed a determination to come, either Pembroke had agreed, or else Madame Koller had followed him—in either case Olivia was not pleased, and received the Colonel's information that the Pembrokes would be there sure in ominous silence. Nothing remained but for her to show what a remarkably good dinner she could give—and this she felt was clearly within her power. She was naturally a clever housekeeper, and as the case often was in those days, the freedom of the negroes had made but little difference in the ménage at Isleham. Most of the house servants had turned squatters on the plantation. Petrarch, unpopular among his confrères because of his superior advantages and accomplishments as well as his assumption of righteousness, was the major-domo—and then there was Ike, a gingerbread colored Chesterfield, as dining-room servant.

"Miss 'Livy, you jes' let me manage dem black niggers," was Petrarch's sensible advice. "Dey doan know nuttin' 'bout a real swell dinner. I say yistiddy to Cook M'ria, 'Why doan yer have some orntrees fur dinner outen all dat chicken an' truck you has lef' over ev'y day?' an' Miss 'Livy, ef you will b'lieve me, dat nigger, she chase me outen de kitchen wid a shovel full o' live coals. She ain' got no 'spect for 'ligion. Arter I got out in de yard, I say, 'You discontemptuous, disreligious ole cantamount, doan' you know better'n to sass de Lord's 'n'inted?'" (this being Petrarch's favorite characterization of himself). "But M'ria ain' got de sperrit 'scusin' 'tis de sperrit o' owdaciousness. Ez fur dat Ike, I done tole him 'I am de Gord o' respication,' an' he 'low I ain't no sech a thing. I gwi'n lick dat yaller nigger fo' long."

"You'd better not try it Uncle Petrarch—" (Petrarch was near to sixty, and was therefore by courtesy, Uncle Petrarch). "Ike won't stand it, and *I* won't have it either, I can tell you."

The Berkeleys went against the county custom, and dined in the evening. Therefore, at seven o'clock precisely, on the evening of the dinner, French

Pembroke and his brother entered the quaint old drawing-room at Isleham. Olivia had learned the possibilities of ancient mahogany furniture and family portraits, and the great rambling old house was picturesque enough. A genuine Virginia wood fire roared up the chimney, where most of the heat as well as the flame went. Wax candles, in tall silver candlesticks, were on the mantel, and the piano. Miss Berkeley herself, in a white wool gown, looked a part of the pleasant home-like picture, as she greeted her two guests. French Pembroke had called twice to see them, but neither time had Olivia been at home. This, then, was their first meeting, except the few minutes at the races. He was the same easy, pleasantly cynical Pembroke she had known in Paris. There was another French Pembroke whom she remembered in her childish days as very good natured, when he was not very tyrannical, in the visits she used to pay with her dead and gone mother long ago to Malvern—and this other Pembroke could recite wonderful poetry out of books, and scare little Miles and herself into delicious spasms of terror by the weird stories he would tell. But Miles had changed in every way. He had been in his earlier boyish days the pet and darling of women, but now he slunk away from the pity in their tender eyes. He had once had a mannish little strut and a way of looking out of his bold blue eyes that made a path for him wherever he chose to tread. But now he shambled in, keeping as far out of sight as possible behind the elder brother's stalwart figure.

Colonel Berkeley shook Miles's one hand cordially. His armless sleeve was pinned up to his coat front.

"God bless my soul," the Colonel cried. "Am I getting old? Here's little Miles Pembroke almost a man."

"Almost—papa—you mean quite a man. It is a dreadful reflection to me that I am older than Miles," said Olivia, smiling. Then they sat about the fire, and Olivia, putting her fan down in her lap, looked French Pembroke full in the face and said, "You know, perhaps, that Madame Koller and Mr. Ahlberg dine here to-night?"

"Yes," answered Pembroke, with all the coolness of conscious innocence—or brazen assurance of careless wickedness, Olivia could not tell which.

"You saw a good deal of them abroad, didn't you?" was her next question.

"Yes," again replied Pembroke.

"Olivia, my dear," said her father, who very much enjoyed this little episode, "you women will never learn that you can't find anything out by asking questions; and Pembroke, my boy, remember that women never believe you except when you are lying to them. Let him alone, Olivia, and he will tell you the whole story, I'll warrant."

Olivia's training had made her something of a stoic under Colonel Berkeley's remarks, but at this a deep red dyed her clear pale face. She was the best of daughters, but she could at that moment have cheerfully inflicted condign punishment on her father. Pembroke saw it too, not without a little malicious satisfaction. She had quietly assumed in her tone and manner that he was in some way responsible for Madame Koller and her mother being at The Beeches—an incident fraught with much discomfort for him—none the less that there was nothing tragic about it, but rather ridiculous. All the same, he determined to set himself right on the spot.

"Of course, I saw them often. It would have been quite unpardonable if I had not, considering we were often in the same places—and our land joins. I can't say that I recollect Madame Koller very much before she went away. I only remember her as rather an ugly little thing, always strumming on the piano. I took the liberty of telling both her and Madame Schmidt that I did not think they would find a winter at The Beeches very pleasant—but it seems she did not agree with me. Ahlberg is a cousin by marriage, and has been in the diplomatic corps—"

And at that very moment Petrarch threw open the drawing-room door and announced "Mrs. Koller and Mr. Ahlberg, sah."

Madame Koller's appearance was none the less striking in evening dress, with ropes of amber around her neck, and some very fine diamonds. Who says that women are indifferent to each other? The instant Olivia beheld Madame Koller in her gorgeous trailing gown of yellow silk, and her jewels, she felt plain, insignificant, and colorless both in features, dress and manner—while Madame Koller, albeit she knew both herself and other women singularly well, almost envied Olivia the girlish simplicity, the slightness and grace that made her a pretty picture in her white gown with the bunch of late autumn roses at her belt.

The clergyman came last. Then Petrarch opened the folding doors and announced dinner, and Colonel Berkeley gallantly offering his arm to Madame Koller, they all marched in.

Something like a sigh of satisfaction escaped Mr. Ahlberg. Once more he was to dine. Madame Koller sat on the Colonel's right, and at her right was Mr. Cole. The clergyman's innocent heart beat when he saw this arrangement. He still fancied that he strongly disapproved of Madame Koller, the more so when he saw the nonchalant way in which she took champagne and utterly ignored the carafe of water at her plate. Mr. Cole took only claret, and watered that liberally.

Madame Koller certainly had a very pretty manner—rather elaborate and altogether different from Olivia's self-possessed simplicity. She spoke of her mother—"so happy once more to be back in Virginia." Madame Schmidt, always wrapped up in shawls, and who never volunteered a remark to anybody in her life, scarcely seemed to outsiders to be quite capable of any enjoyment. And Aunt Peyton—dear Aunt Peyton—so kind, so handsome—so anxious that people shall please themselves—"Upon my soul, madam," cried the Colonel, with much hearty good humor, "I am delighted to hear that last about my old friend Sally Peyton. I've known her well for fifty years—perhaps she wouldn't acknowledge it—and a more headstrong, determined, self-willed woman I never saw. Sally is a good woman, and by heaven, she was a devilish pretty one when—when—you may have heard the story, ma'am—but she always wanted to please herself a d—n sight more than anybody else—including Ned Peyton."

The Colonel said this quite pleasantly, and Madame Koller smiled at it—she seldom laughed. "Were you not some years in the army, Colonel Berkeley?" she asked presently. "It seems to me I have some recollection of having heard it." Colonel Berkeley colored slightly. He valued his military title highly, but he didn't know exactly how he came by it.

"The fact is madam," he replied, clearing his throat, "in the old days we had a splendid militia. Don't you remember the general musters, hay? Now I was the—the commanding officer of the Virginia Invincibles—a crack cavalry company, composed exclusively of the county gentlemen—and in some way, they called me colonel, and a colonel I remained."

"The title seems quite natural," said Madame Koller, with a sweet smile—"You have such a military carriage—that indescribable air—" at which the Colonel, who never tired of laughing at other people's foibles, straightened up, assumed a martial pose, and showed vast elation and immense pleasure—which Madame Koller saw out of the corner of her eye.

Miles, sitting next Olivia, had grown confidential. "I—I—want to tell you," he said bashfully, "the reason why I didn't come to see you in Paris. It required some nerve for a fellow—in my condition—to face a woman—even the best and kindest."

"Was that it?" answered Olivia half smiling.

"You are laughing at me," he said reproachfully.

"Of course I am," replied Olivia.

A genuine look of relief stole into his poor face. Perhaps it was not so bad after all if Olivia Berkeley could laugh at his sensitiveness.

"So," continued Olivia, promptly, "you acted like a vain, foolish boy. But I see you are getting over it."

"I'll try. You wouldn't treat me so cavalierly, would you, if—if—it were quite—dreadful?"

"No, it isn't dreadful at all, or anything like it," replied Olivia, telling one of those generous and womanly fibs that all true women utter with the full approval of their consciences.

Meanwhile, Ahlberg and Pembroke had been conversing. Ahlberg was indeed a clever fellow—for he talked in a straightforward way, and gave not the slightest ground in anything he said for the suspicion that Pembroke obstinately cherished against him.

"What do you do with yourself all day, Miss Berkeley?" asked Pembroke after a while.

"There is plenty to do. I have a dozen servants to manage that ran wild while we were away—and the house to keep, and to look after the garden—and I ride or drive every day—and keep up my piano playing—and read a little. What do you do?"

"Nothing," answered Pembroke, boldly.

Olivia did not say a word. She threw him one brief glance though, from her dark eyes that conveyed a volume.

"I have a license to practice law," he continued, coolly. "I've had it for five years—got it just before the State went out, when I went out too. Four years' soldiering isn't a good preparation for the law."

"Ah!" said Olivia.

"I have enough left, I daresay, to keep me without work," he added.

If he had studied how to make himself contemptible in Olivia's eyes, he could not have done so more completely. She had acquired perfect self-possession of manner, but her mobile face was as yet undisciplined. When to this last remark she said in her sweetest manner, "Won't you let Petrarch fill your glass?" it was equivalent to saying, "You are the most worthless and contemptible creature on this planet." Just then the Colonel's cheery voice resounded from the foot of the table.

"Pembroke, when I drove through the Court House to-day, it made me feel like a young man again, to see your father's old tin sign hanging out of the old office, 'French Pembroke, Attorney at Law.' It has been a good many years since that sign was first put up. Egad, your father and I have had some good times in that office, in the old, old days. He always kept a first-class brand of liquors. His style of serving it wasn't very imposing, but it didn't hurt the liquor. I've drank cognac fit for a king in that office, and drank it out of a shaving mug borrowed from the barber next door—ha! ha!"

A change like magic swept over Olivia's face. It indicated great relief that Pembroke was not an idle scamp after all. She tried to look sternly and reproachfully at him, but a smile lurked in her eyes.

"You are not as lazy as I thought you, but twice as deceitful," she said.

Pembroke was amused at the extreme suavity of the two ladies toward each other, knowing that at heart it masked an armed neutrality. Particularly did he notice it after dinner, when they returned to the drawing-room and the piano was opened. Madame Koller was asked to sing, but first begged that Miss Berkeley should play. Olivia, without protesting, went to the piano. Her playing was finished and artistic, and full of the delicate repose of a true musician. When she rose Madame Koller overflowed with compliments. "And now, madam," said the Colonel, rising and offering his hand with a splendid and graceful flourish, "will you not let us hear that voice that charmed us when you were little Eliza Peyton?"

Madame Koller did not like to be called Eliza Peyton—it was too commonplace—Elise Koller was much more striking. And then she was uncertain whether to sing or not. She had tried hard to keep that stage episode secret, and she was afraid if she sang, that something might betray her. She glanced at Ahlberg, as much as to say, "Shall I?" but Ahlberg maintained a sphinx-like gravity. But the temptation was too great. Olivia's playing was pretty for an amateur—but Madame Koller despised the best amateur performance as only a true professional can. Therefore she rose and went to the piano, and turned over some of the ballads there. She pretended to be looking at them, but she was not.

"Louis," she said to Ahlberg, who was twisting his waxed mustache. He came at once and seated himself at the piano.

"What do you think of '*Caro nome?*'" she asked.

"Very good. You always sung the *Rigoletto* music well."

Madame Koller was not pleased at this slip—but at all events, nobody but herself understood it in the sense that Ahlberg meant.

Ahlberg struck a few chords, and Madame Koller begun from memory the celebrated aria. As she sang, Colonel Berkeley opened his sharp old eyes very wide indeed. This was not the kind of music often heard in drawing-rooms. He glanced at Pembroke, to see if he was astonished. That young gentleman only leaned back in the sofa corner near the fire to better enjoy this delicious singing. Olivia's face looked puzzled—so did Miles. In singing, Madame Koller was handsomer than ever. She had perfect control over her facial expression, and seemed quite transformed. Once or twice she used a graceful gesture, or made a step forward—it was highly dramatic, but not in the least stagy.

But if Madame Koller's performance was far out of the common run, so was that of her accompanist. He looked remarkably at home on the piano stool, and Colonel Berkeley rubbed his eyes and tried to recall if he had ever seen Ahlberg ornamenting a piano stool at a concert, but could not remember. When the last brilliant note and rich chord died away Miles Pembroke suddenly began to clap his knee loudly with his one remaining hand—which produced a furious hand clapping, in which everybody else vehemently and involuntarily joined, Mr. Cole feebly shouting "Bravo! Bravo!" Madame Koller started, and when the applause ceased, she seemed like one coming out of a dream. In the buzz of compliments that followed, Ahlberg's voice cut in saying, "You were too dramatic."

Madame Koller had been receiving the compliments paid her with smiling grace, but at this, she cast a strange look on Ahlberg, nor would she sing again, although urged to do so. And presently it was time to leave, and Madame Koller and her escort departed in the little victoria which had come for them, the Colonel wrapping her up in innumerable furs to protect her from the sharp night air of November.

When he returned to the drawing-room, Olivia and the clergyman and the Pembrokes were all standing around the blazing fire. The Colonel walked in, and squaring himself before the generous fireplace with his coat tails over his arm, surveyed the company and remarked,

"Professional, by Jove."

"Now, papa," said Olivia, taking him by the arm, "you are the best and kindest of men, but you shan't say 'professional, by Jove,' of Madame Koller, the very minute she has quitted your house. You know how often I've told you of my rule that you shall not mention the name of a guest until twenty-four hours after that guest's departure."

She said it with an air of authority, and tweaked the Colonel's ear to emphasize her severity.

"But I am not saying any harm about her, Olivia."

"Just what I expected," groaned Mr. Cole.

"Perhaps her voice gave out, and she quitted the stage early," remarked Pembroke.

"Not a word more," cried Olivia sternly. "She sings delightfully. But—a—it *was* rather prima donna-ish."

"Aha! Oho!" shouted the Colonel. "There you are, my dear!"

CHAPTER IV.

A WEEK or two after the dinner at Isleham, Pembroke sat in his office, one afternoon, at the county-seat, with a letter spread out before him. It was very thumbed and illiterate, and quite devoid of punctuation.

"Marse french, i is in a heap of truble marse french an i aint done nuttin—i bought ten akers fum mr. Hackett you know mr. hackett he some relation to dem Hibbses he come frum i donow whar an he allus cussin de yankees an I had done pay him fur de ten akers mos all i had done got married ter Jane you know Jane whar was Miss livia Berkeley maid, an mr. hackett he come an he say he was gwine take the baid an he call me a low down nigger and kase I arnser him he hit me wid he stick an marse french i couldn't help it an he hit Jane too an i knock him down an o marse french he went home an naix day he die an de sheriff he come an put me in jail—i feerd dey gwine hang me like a hound dog i aint got no money fur lawyers, an mr. hackett's folks dem Hibbses dey is engage all de lawyers i dunno what i gwine do if you doan cum home to try me marse french—you know i was yur vally an daddy he was ole marse's vally, an me an you useter go fishin when we was small an ole marse useter lick bofe on us fur gittin drownded in de crick i carn sleep at night, not kase de bed is hard an de straw cum thu de tickin but kase i feerd dey gwine ter hang me like a hound dog de black folks is agin me kase mr. hackett was fum de norf an de white folks is agin me kase mr. hackett was white o marse french fur Gord Amighty's sake come long home and doan let em hang me Jane she is mighty poly an carn cum to see me sum gentmun swar at me you aint never done it—you give me a quarter evry time I hol yo horse No mo now from

"bob henry."

This letter had reached him in Paris, and had more to do with bringing him home just when he came than Madame Koller—much more than Madame Koller expected—or Olivia, either, for that matter.

"It is a rather hard case," he thought to himself, with a grim smile, "a man can't go and say, 'See what a disinterested thing I have done: come home months before I intended, to defend a poor ragged black rascal that claimed to be my "vally," and expects to be hanged—and half the county believes I came in obedience to Madame Koller.'" But it occurred to him that he had done a good deal to make both Olivia Berkeley and Madame Koller believe what was not true about his return.

He put on his hat and, putting the letter in his pocket, went out and mounted his horse and rode off at a smart canter away from the village, down a little-used road, until he came to a stretch of pine woods. Then, following a bridle path a mile or more, he came upon a log house.

Everything had an air of sylvan peace in the quiet autumn afternoon. There was nothing to indicate domestic life about the place—the persons who lived within had no garden, no fowls—nothing but the log cabin under the pines. Pembroke knocked loudly with the butt of his riding whip at the rude door, but a voice a little way off answered him.

"Don't waste your strength on the portcullis of the castle. Here I am."

Pembroke followed the sound, leading his horse, and in a minute or two came upon a man of middle age, lying full length on the soft bed of pine needles, with a book and a pipe.

"This is peaceful," said Pembroke, after tethering his horse and seating himself. "At Malvern it is more lonely than peaceful. The house is so large and so empty—Miles and I live in one wing of it. It wasn't half a bad thing for you, Cave, when the doctors ordered you to the pine woods."

Cave nodded.

"It's uncommonly quiet and peaceful, this camping out. As I have no other house to go to, since mine was burned down, it rather bridges over the gulf of appearances to say I am living in a log cabin by command of the most mighty Dr. Sam Jones."

"And there is no loneliness like that of a half deserted house," continued Pembroke, unconsciously dropping his voice in sympathy with the faint woodland murmur around them. "It seems to me at Malvern that I continually hear my mother's voice, and my father's footstep, and all the pleasant family commotion I remember. And Elizabeth—Cave, no woman I ever knew suffered like my sister—and she was not the woman to suffer patiently. Old Keturah tells me that my father would have yielded at any time after he saw that her heart and life were bound up in Waring—but she would not ask him—so while I was enjoying myself three thousand miles away, and only sad when I came home to Miles, Elizabeth and my father were fighting that dreary battle. Keturah says that everybody said she was sweetly and gently patient, but all night she would walk the floor sobbing and weeping, while my father below walked his floor. It killed them both."

Cave had turned away his head. Who has watched one, dearly loved, waste and die for another, without knowing all there is of bitterness? And was Pembroke so forgetful? He was not, indeed—but he had begun telling of the things which troubled him, and because he could bear to speak of poor Elizabeth he thought that Cave could bear to hear it. But there was a pause—a pause in which Pembroke suddenly felt ashamed and heartless.

Elizabeth's death was much to him—but it was everything to Cave. So Pembroke continued, rather to excuse himself, "Your cabin in the woods is at least not haunted by the dead people you loved. Sometimes, when I go into my mother's room and see everything as she left it—the mirror in which I have often seen her braid her hair—she had scarcely a gray lock in it when she died—I feel—I cannot describe to you what I feel."

"You ought to marry," remarked Cave, in a cold, quiet voice.

"Not I," answered Pembroke, carelessly, glad to escape from the train he had himself started. "I suppose a man ought to marry some time or other—but forty is early enough. I wouldn't mind waiting until I were fifty. At sixty a man is apt to make an infernal fool of himself."

"How about Eliza Peyton—or Madame Koller—whom you followed here?"

Pembroke had lighted a cigar since they began talking, and had disposed of himself comfortably on the pine needles by the side of his friend. The silence was the unbroken silence of the autumn woods. There was not the faintest whisper of wind, but over their heads the solemn trees leaned together and rustled softly. A long pause came after Cave's question. Into Pembroke's sunburnt face a dark flush slowly mounted. It is not often that a man of his type, with his iron jaw and strong features, blushes—but this was a blush of consciousness, though not of shame.

"I did not follow her here," he said. "But who believes me? I think the woman herself fancies I did follow her. As for that little haughty Olivia Berkeley, the girl gives me a look that is equivalent to a box on the ear every time Madame Koller is mentioned. If ever I marry, I shan't take a woman of spirit, you may depend upon it. I shall take a placid, stout creature. An eaglet like Olivia Berkeley is well enough for a man to amuse himself with—but for steady matrimony give me a barnyard fowl."

"God help you," answered Cave piously.

"But what really brought me here—although I knew all the time that I ought not to be loitering in Europe, and would probably have come anyhow—was this poor devil, Bob Henry, in jail, charged with murdering Hackett, that scalawag the Hibbses brought here."

At this Cave sat up, full of animation.

"I can help the poor fellow, I think," he said. "I went to see him as soon as they put him in jail—a wretched looking object in rags he was, too. He seemed to put great faith in you, and I did not tell him of some evidence that I have got hold of. The fellow's going to get clear between us, I think."

Pembroke sat up too, and took the cigar out of his mouth. The lawyer's instinct rose within him, and he took to his profession like a pointer to his field work.

"You see, having been away during Hackett's time, I know nothing of his habits or associations except from hearsay. Any lawyer in the county could do better for poor Bob Henry than I—in that way."

"Hackett, you know, was a Northern man, who came down here and bought property during the war. He was a rabid Southerner. I distrusted the man for that alone. He was related to our friends, the Hibbses. I always suspected he had something to do with that gang of deserters down by the river, and if he was not a spy, then John Cave is a fool."

"Well—what else?"

"Of course you know about Bob Henry's buying the land of him, and the money he owed him, and the fight. The negro, after Hackett had struck him and insulted his wife, struck him back with a stick. Now the Hibbses, and everybody else for that matter, think that blow killed him. You see, among the people Hackett had a kind of false popularity, as a Northern man who has espoused Southern sentiments—a hypocrite, in short. The feeling against that poor black wretch was savage."

"So," said Pembroke, "instead of proving that the blow did kill Hackett, the jury will want it proved that it didn't kill Hackett."

"Exactly."

"Hackett, I understand, was a convivial soul. It can be proved that he mounted his horse, rode home, and six hours afterward was walking about. It never seemed to occur to these country doctors to look for any other injury than the bruise on the head, when they found him as good as dead next morning. I hear, though, that people who passed his house at night would often hear shouting and carousing. Now, who did that shouting and carousing? Not the gentlemen in the county, certainly, nor anybody else that I can find out. This fits in with your account of his associating with deserters. I have always had a theory that he received an injury that killed him between the time he was seen alive and apparently well, and when he was found dying in his bed."

"That is precisely what I think—and I have a witness, a ragged boy, hereabouts, whom I have tried to keep respectable, who heard a great noise as of men shouting and drinking at Hackett's house the night of Hackett's death. The boy was cold and hungry, and although he knew he would be driven away if caught—for Hackett was a hard-hearted villain—yet he sneaked up to the house and gazed through the half-drawn curtains at the men sitting around the table, fascinated as he says by the sight of fire and food. He heard Hackett singing and laughing, and he saw the faces, and—mark you,—knows the names of those low fellows, who have never been suspected, and who have kept so remarkably quiet. Then, here is the point—one of the very men who deserted from my company, and was very thick afterward with Hackett, suddenly disappeared, and within a month died of injuries he could give no account of. You may depend upon it they had a fight, and it was my former companion in arms that killed the worthy Hackett—not poor Bob Henry's blow."

Pembroke's dark eyes shone.

"We'll keep this to ourselves, and make the fellow hold his tongue. We won't give the deserters a chance to concoct a plausible lie. They will be certain to be at the court house when the trial comes off, and when I put them in the witness box unprepared—you will see."

They talked over the case a half an hour longer before Pembroke got up to go. Then he said: "Are you going to call at The Beeches? You must have known Eliza Koller before she left here."

"Know her," cried Cave, "yes, I know her. I hope she has improved in every other way as much as she has in looks. I saw her the other day. It seemed to me that her hair was not so violently yellow when she went away; however, I'll be cautious,—I see you are badly singed. Little Olivia Berkeley wouldn't do for my lord—"

Pembroke got up and flung off in a passion, pursued by Cave shouting:

"I'll give long odds on the widow!"

CHAPTER V.

A FEW Sundays after that, Mr. Cole's heart was gladdened by the sight of Madame Koller and the bundle of cloaks and mufflers she called her mamma, walking in church just as the morning service was beginning. The little clergyman felt inspired. He fancied himself like Paul before the Athenians. Olivia Berkeley was there too, and the Colonel, who settled himself in his pew to catch Mr. Cole in a false syllogism or a misquotation—anything to chaff the reverend gentleman about during the coming week. Mr. Cole did his best. He laid aside his manuscript and indulged in an extempore address that warmed the orator, if not the congregation, with something like eloquence. The Hibbses were there too—a florid, well-dressed family, Mr. Hibbs making the responses in a basso so much louder than Mr. Cole's mild treble that it seemed as if Mr. Hibbs were the parson and Mr. Cole the clerk.

"I tell you what it is my dear," Colonel Berkeley had said angrily to his daughter half an hour before when the Hibbses swept past them up the flagged walk through the churchyard, "the religion of these infernal Hibbs people is what disgusts me most. They made their money in the war of 1812. Up to then they were shouting Methodists—I've heard my father swear it a hundred times—" The Colonel belonged to a class, not uncommon in Virginia, who regarded the Episcopal Church as a close corporation, and resented with great pugnacity any attempt to enter it on the part of the great unwashed. It was the vehicle chosen by the first families to go to heaven in, and marked "Reserved." Hence the Colonel's wrath. His church was a church founded by gentlemen, of gentlemen, and for gentlemen, and it was a great liberty for any other class to seek that aristocratic mode of salvation.

"Now, damme, the Hibbses are the greatest Episcopalians in the parish. I am as good a churchman as there is in the county, but begad, if I want such a set of vulgarians worshiping under the same roof and rubbing elbows with me when I go up to the Lord's table. I think I gave that young Hibbs fellow a setback last communion Sunday which will prevent him from hustling up to the rail before his betters."

By which it will be seen that Dashaway's unlucky fiasco and the triumph of the long-legged roan at Campdown had not been obliterated from the Colonel's memory. During the sermon, Colonel Berkeley only took his eyes off the clergyman once. This was when Mr. Hibbs came around with the collection plate. The object of that day's collection was, as Mr. Cole had feelingly stated, for the conversion of the higher castes in India. Colonel

Berkeley thrust both hands in his trousers' pockets, and surveyed Mr. Hibbs defiantly as that worthy citizen poked the plate at him. This duello between Mr. Hibbs and Colonel Berkeley occurred every collection Sunday, to the edification of the congregation. After holding the plate before the Colonel for a considerable time, Mr. Hibbs moved off—a time that seemed interminable to Olivia, blushing furiously in the corner of the pew.

After church the congregation streamed out, and according to the country custom, the people stopped to talk in the churchyard. Colonel Berkeley marched up to Mr. Cole, and put something in his hand.

"There, Cole," he remarked, "I wouldn't put anything in the plate when that ruffian of a vestry-man of yours poked it under my nose. But I doubled my contribution, and I'll thank you to put it with the rest."

"Certainly, Colonel," answered Mr. Cole—"but Christian charity—"

"Christian charity be hanged, sir. I'm a Christian and a churchman, but I prefer Christian gentlemen to Methodist upstarts. Whether I go to heaven or the other place either, damme, I propose to go in good company."

"This will go to the missionary fund for India, Colonel."

"Ha! ha! I'd like to see one of you callow young clergymen tackle a Brahmin in India. By Jove. It would be fun—for the Brahmin!"

Colonel Berkeley had no mind to let Mr. Cole monopolize Madame Koller, so just as the clergyman stood, hat in hand bowing to her and her mother, the Colonel marched up, and by a skillful maneuver shoveled the elder lady off on Mr. Cole, while he himself attended the younger one to the carriage. At the churchyard gate was Olivia Berkeley talking with Mrs. Peyton—and by her side stood French Pembroke. Madame Koller smiled charmingly at her old acquaintances. She was so sorry Miss Berkeley had not been at home the day she called. Miss Berkeley was politely regretful. It was so sunshiny and delightful that Madame Koller would like to walk as far as the main road led them toward home—it was only across a field or two then, for each of them to reach home. Olivia also assented to this. Madame Koller's society was far from lacking charm to her—and besides, the attraction of repulsion is never stronger than between two women who cherish a smoldering spark of jealousy.

Madame Koller wanted the Colonel to come, and brought her whole battery of smiles and glances into action to compel him—but he got out of it with much astuteness. He was no walker, he said. Then she turned to French Pembroke.

"Good-bye, my dear," said Mrs. Peyton to Olivia, *sotto voce*. "Don't be left at the meeting of the ways."

"No, I won't, I promise you," replied Olivia.

Off they started. Madame Koller moved with the grace of a fairy in a drawing-room, but on a country road, holding a sunshade in one hand and her gown in the other, it was a promenade rather than a walk. Olivia walked with the easy step of a girl country born and country bred, and albeit it was a little more than a saunter, she soon walked Madame Koller out of breath.

Pembroke had but little share in the conversation. Except a laughing reference to him occasionally, he was left out, and had full opportunity to compare the two women—which he did with an amused smile. Compliments were plenty from Madame Koller, which Olivia deftly parried or ignored. In a little while the turning was in sight where both left the high road, and a path in one direction led to Isleham, and in another, gave a short cut to The Beeches. Pembroke was beginning to apprehend an awkward predicament for himself as to which one of the ladies he should accompany, when Olivia cut the knot.

"Here I must leave you—good-bye, Madame Koller, I shall see you during the week—good-bye—" to Pembroke.

"There is Madame Koller's carriage in sight," remarked Pembroke, thinking that offered a solution of the problem—to which Olivia only responded pleasantly—"Good-bye—good-bye—" and tripped off.

Madame Koller looked rather foolish—she had been outgeneraled completely.

"There is your carriage," again said Pembroke, this time looking straight at her.

"Yes. I know it. You will soon be rid of me."

As she spoke her eyes filled with real tears of mortification. Pembroke was a man, and he could not see this, and be as hard as he meant to be. Nevertheless, he did not intend to walk through the field with Madame Koller.

"Come, Elise," he said. "The way is too long for you. You are no walker. It would be best for you to drive home."

"When you call me Elise I will do anything for you," she said—and she was really tired and hated walking for walking's sake.

The carriage drew up, and Pembroke put her in carefully. Old Madame Schmidt said: "That is right, Eliza," and they drove off.

A few yards hid him from their sight, and at that instant he struck out in the path to Isleham. In ten minutes he had overtaken Olivia.

She was surprised to see him.

"What have you done with Madame Koller?"

"Put her in the carriage and sent her home."

A faint flush crept into Olivia's cheeks.

"I have wanted to ask you something for a week or two," she said, "but this is my first opportunity. You know that poor negro, Bob Henry, who is to be tried for murder—I believe he belonged to you, didn't he?"

"Yes."

"His wife was my maid when I was a child. Yesterday she came to see me—just out of her bed from a long fever. She is naturally in great trouble about her husband, whom she has not seen, the jail being too far off. She has heard something about your defending him when he is tried, and she begged me to see you, and ask you as a mercy to them, to 'try him,' as she says."

"That is what brought me back to America," he replied.

Olivia said not a word, but walked on. She could not but believe him—but if he had not come on Madame Koller's account, Madame Koller might have come on his account.

"I have done, and I am doing, the best I can for the poor fellow. Cave has helped me much."

Then it occurred to Olivia that at least Pembroke ought to get the credit for coming on such an errand.

"How kind it was of you," she said. "I am so glad—"

"To find I am not such a scamp as you thought me?" he said, good-naturedly.

"Have it any way you like," she replied. "But I am very glad, and Jane will be very glad, and I'm sure Bob Henry is—and you may come home with me and have some luncheon, and papa will be very glad—he hates Sunday afternoons in the country."

CHAPTER VI.

MEANWHILE poor Mr. Ahlberg, condemned to the solitude of the village tavern, varied by daily visits to The Beeches and occasional ones to his acquaintances, the Pembrokes and the Berkeleys, found life tedious. He wanted to get away, but Madame Koller would not let him. Mr. Ahlberg had now, for some years, had an eye to Madame Koller's fortune. Therefore, when she commanded him to stay, he stayed. He regarded her infatuation for Pembroke as a kind of temporary insanity, which would in time be cured, and that he would be the physician and would marry his patient afterward.

As for Madame Koller, she was wretched, anxious, everything but bored. That she was not—she was too miserable. Like Ahlberg, she thought herself almost a lunatic. Hers was not the folly of a guileless girl, but the deep-seated and unspeakable folly of a matured woman. When M. Koller died she had regarded herself as one of the most fortunate women in the world. Still young, rich, pretty, what more could she ask? The world had almost forgotten, if it ever knew, that she had had a stage career, when stage careers were not the most desirable things in the world. She had done her duty as well as she knew it by the dead and gone Koller, who, in consideration of leaving her a comfortable fortune, had made her life a torment upon earth. Just when she was preparing to enjoy her liberty she had found herself enslaved by her own act as it were. Sometimes she asked herself contemptuously what Pembroke could give her if she married him, in exchange for liberty which she prized, and answered herself with the wisdom of the world. Again she reasoned with herself and got for answer the wildest folly a girl of sixteen could imagine. With him was everything—without him was nothing. And his indifference piqued her. She truly believed him quite callous to any woman, and she had often heard him say that he had no intention of marrying. Pembroke, returning to the life of a country gentleman after four years' campaigning, followed by a time of thoughtless pleasure, mixed with the pain of defeat, of the misery of seeing Miles forever wretched, broken in fortune, though not in spirit, found Madame Koller's society quite fascinating enough. But he was not so far gone that he did not see the abyss before him. On the one hand was money and luxury and pleasure and idleness and Madame Koller, with her blonde hair and her studied graces and her dramatic singing—and on the other was work and perhaps poverty, and a dull provincial existence. But then he would be a man—and if he married Madame Koller he would not be a man. It is no man's part to live solely for any woman, and nobody knew that better than French Pembroke. Of course, he knew that he could marry her—the love-making, such as it was, had been chiefly on the lady's part. He was angry beyond measure with her when she appeared upon the scene. He wished to try life without Madame Koller. But when she came she certainly drew him often to The Beeches. There was but one other woman in the county who really interested him. This was Olivia Berkeley, and she was uncertain and hard to please. It was undeniably pleasant to ride over to The Beeches on winter afternoons and find Madame Koller in a cosy sitting room before a wood fire, and to have her read to him and sing to him. Sometimes he wondered how he ever came away unpledged. Again, he faintly blamed himself for going—but if he remained away Madame Koller sent for him and reproached him bitterly. She knew quite as much of the world as he did—and he was no mean proficient—and was two or three years older than he besides. But it was an unsatisfactory existence to him. He felt when he went from Madame Koller's presence into Olivia's like going from a ball room out into the clear moonlit night. To be on his guard always against a woman, to try and make the best of an anomalous condition, was offensive to his naturally straightforward mind. It relieved him to be with Olivia, even though occasionally she treated him cavalierly. This last he positively relished as a luxury.

Ahlberg he hated. Yet they were scrupulously polite to each other, and Ahlberg occasionally dined with him at Malvern.

One day he met Ahlberg in the road near the village. Ahlberg had a gun and a full game-bag slung over his shoulder.

"You have had good luck," said Pembroke.

"Very," answered Ahlberg, with his peculiar smile. "I saw nothing to shoot, but I met two blacks, and for a trifle I bought all this. I am not a sportsman like you. I go for a walk—I take my gun. I want a few birds for an entrée. It matters very little where I get them."

"What we call a pot hunter," remarked Pembroke, laughing at what he considered great simplicity on Ahlberg's part. For his own part, his instincts of sport made him consider Ahlberg's method of securing an entrée as but little better than sheep stealing. Ahlberg did not quite take in what manner of sport pot hunting was, nor the contumely visited upon a pot hunter, and so was not offended.

"Will you not come to The Beeches to-morrow evening and dine with us on these birds?" he asked. "This is *my* party, not Elise's, who is ill with a distressing cold. I have asked the Reverend Cole too, and Hibbs and some others, and we will have a 'jollitime' as you Americans and English say."

Pembroke agreed, he scarcely knew why, particularly as he seldom dined at The Beeches, and never before at Ahlberg's invitation.

Next evening therefore with Mr. Cole and Mr. Hibbs and young Peyton and two or three others Pembroke found himself in the great, gloomy dining room at The Beeches. Neither Madame Koller nor Madame Schmidt were present. The cold was a real cold. Madame Koller was on the sofa in her sitting room, and if she felt strong enough, sent word to the guests she would see them in the drawing-room later on. The round table though, in the middle of the room, looked cheerful enough, and on the sideboard was an array of long-necked bottles such as Pembroke had never seen for so small a party.

Ahlberg was an accomplished diner out—but that is something different from a good diner at home. He was graceful and attentive, but he lacked altogether the Anglo-Saxon good fellowship. He tucked a napkin under his chin, discussed ménus with much gravity, and referred too often to Hans, a nondescript person whom Madame Koller had brought from Vienna, and who was cook, butler, major-domo and valet in one—and highly accomplished in all. Pembroke was rather disgusted with too much conversation of this sort:

"Hans, you are too pronounced with your truffles. There should be a hint—a mere suspicion—"

"Yes, monsieur. But madame likes truffles. Every day it is 'Hans, you are too sparing of your truffles.'"

"This salmi is really charming. Hans, I shall put it down in my note book."

"I can give monsieur admirable salmis of pigeons as well as duck."

Pembroke, impelled by a spirit of perverseness, declined everything Ahlberg and Hans united in praising, and confined himself solely to port, a wine he did not much care for, and which both Ahlberg and Hans reprobated in the strongest terms.

Not so Mr. Cole. He went religiously through the ménu, praising and exclaiming, and keeping up a fusillade of compliments like the chorus in a Greek play. Nor did he forget the long-necked bottles. At first he positively declined anything but claret. But obeying a look from Ahlberg, Hans filled the clergyman's glass with champagne. Mr. Cole laughed and blushed, but on being good naturedly rallied by his companions, especially Mr. Hibbs, he consented to one—only one glass. But this was followed by a second, poured out when Mr. Cole was looking another way—and presently as Hans by degrees slyly filled the half dozen wine glasses at his plate, Mr.

Cole began with an air of perfect unconsciousness to taste them all. Soon his face flushed, and by the time the dinner was half over, Mr. Cole was half over the line of moderation too. He became convivial, and even affectionate. Pembroke, who had looked on the little clergyman's first glass of champagne with a smile, began to feel sorry for him, and a very profound contempt for his entertainer. Hans and his pseudo-master evidently understood each other, and exchanged glances oftener than master and man usually do. As the clergyman became more free in his talk, Ahlberg looked at Pembroke with a foxy smile, but received only a cool stare in return. Pembroke was a jolly companion enough, but this deliberately making a gentleman, weak as he might be, but still a gentleman, drunk in a woman's house struck him as not the most amusing thing in the world. Ahlberg, however, seemed to enjoy the state of affairs, and though he had no sympathy from Pembroke or young Peyton, Mr. Hibbs and one or two others appreciated it highly.

"Ah, Mr. Cole," he cried, "you know how to dine, I see you do. You would not discredit the Trois Frères itself. Hans, more Chablis."

Poor Cole's eyes twinkled. He loved to be thought a man of the world.

"Couldn't you give us a song, Mr. Cole?" continued Ahlberg, laughing, "English and American fashion, you know. Something about wine and mirth."

Mr. Cole smiled coquettishly, and cleared his throat.

"Perhaps I might try 'The Heart Bowed Down With Weight of Woe,'" said he.

"Yes—yes—"

"Or, 'Then You'll Remember Me.' That's more sentimental—more suited for the occasion."

"'Then You'll Remember Me,' by all means. Gentlemen, a chorus."

Mr. Cole, placing his hand upon his heart, after having drained another glass of champagne, began in a weak and rather shaky voice,

"'When other lips and other hearts

Their tales of love shall tell.'

"Gentlemen, I'm not in good voice to-night.

"'In language whose excess imparts

The power they feel so well;

When hollow hearts shall wear a mask,'

"Here, Hans, old boy, I'll take another glass of Chablis—

"''Twill break your own to see,

In such a moment I but a—a—a—sk

That you'll remember me.'"

Here a tremendous chorus, led by Mr. Ahlberg, broke in, accompanied with much pounding on the table, and a rhythmic jingling of glasses:

"Then you'll remember me, boys,

Then you'll remember me."

Mr. Cole, very much annoyed and preposterously dignified, began to protest.

"Gentlemen—er—beloved brethren, I mean gentlemen, this song is a sentimental one—a sentimental song, d'ye hear—and does not admit of a convivial chorus. Now, I'll give you the last verse over."

Mr. Cole, looking lackadaisically at the ceiling, began again. When he reached the last line, again an uproarious chorus took the words out of his mouth. He rose, and steadying himself on his feet, implored silence in pantomime. In vain. Ahlberg and Hibbs with shouts and yells of laughter carried the chorus through. Pembroke could not but laugh, but he said to the little clergyman, in a tone subdued but authoritative:

"Sit down, Cole."

Mr. Cole glanced fiercely at him. "Were it not for my cloth, sir, you—you'd—receive personal chastisement for that remark," he responded angrily; but comparing his own slender figure with Pembroke's length and strength, he plaintively continued:

"But I'm afraid you could lick me, Pembroke. You always did at school, you know."

Pembroke made no reply. He was no anchorite. He had sometimes found amusement in low company in low places—but low company in better places disgusted him. Besides, Cole was an honest little fellow, and not half such a fool as he appeared—and he had a conscience, and Pembroke began to feel sorry already for the pain poor Cole would have to endure.

But Cole was not the only subject of amusement. Ahlberg, now that his dinner was over, considered conversation in order—and began to give his views on things in general, upon which young Hibbs and young Peyton and the others hung with delight. Pembroke therefore thinking it well to get Cole out of the way while he could yet walk, suggested that he should escape for a breath of fresh air—to which Cole assented, and might have slipped out unnoticed, but for his assumption of a lofty stride, which would have landed him on the floor but for a timely arm from Hans.

The fun grew fast and furious, and everybody at the table was flushed except Ahlberg and Pembroke. Ahlberg drank as much as anybody, but his delicate hand was as steady, and his cold blue eyes as clear as if it had been water from the well he was drinking. Pembroke did not drink much and remained cool and smiling.

After an hour or two had passed, he began to be intensely bored by Mr. Hibbs' songs, who now became the minstrel, Ahlberg's long stories and young Peyton's jokes—and besides he wondered at Mr. Cole's absence. So in the midst of a lively discussion, he quietly left his seat and went out.

In the hall several doors opened—but from the drawing-room door came a flood of light, and voices. He heard Madame Koller's somewhat shrill tones saying:

"But Mr. Cole, I cannot marry you—fancy me—"

"Darling Eliza," cried Mr. Cole, in a maudlin, tipsy voice. "I know you love me. Your partiality—"

Pembroke made two strides to the door. Just as he reached it, he saw a tableau. Mr. Cole, whose head just reached to Madame Koller's shoulder, had seized her by the waist and was saying:

"One kiss—only one, my darling!"

Madame Koller raised her hand—it was large and strong and white—and brought it down upon the clergyman's cheek with a thundering whack that would have knocked him down, but for another slap she administered on the other side. Pembroke had not been in time to save him, but he caught Cole by the collar, and picking him up as if he had been a baby, set him out of the way.

Madame Koller was raging. She stamped her foot and clinched her hands and ground her teeth with passion.

"Come, Madame Koller," said Pembroke, sternly, "there is no occasion for this sort of thing. The little fool is tipsy—of course you see it. You ought not to have had anything to say to him."

But Madame Koller would not be pacified. It was not the liberty he had tried to take which most infuriated her, she inadvertently declared, but the idea that she, Elise Koller, would marry a country parson. She raved. What! She, Elise Koller, born a Peyton, should condescend to that ridiculous person? What would her aunt, Sally Peyton, say to it? What would the shade of the departed Koller say to it? She had been civil to him, and forsooth, he had come, like a thief in the night, and proposed to marry her—her, who might have married a duke—a prince—anybody. Madame Koller was very mad, and used just the extravagant and hysterical language that people of her type do sometimes.

As for Mr. Cole, those two slaps had sobered him as instantly and as completely as anything could. He sat bolt upright on the sofa, while Pembroke with a half smile of contempt in his face that really exasperated Madame Koller more than poor Cole had done, listened to her tirade. What a virago the woman was, to be sure. But how handsome she was too!

"Pembroke," said poor Cole, rising and coming forward, looking quite pale and desperate, "don't try to excuse me. I don't deserve any excuse. I mean to write to the bishop to-morrow and make a clean breast of it—and any punishment he may inflict, or any mortification I may have to endure because of this, I'll take like a man. Madame Koller, I humbly ask your pardon. I hardly knew what I was doing."

"To get drunk in my house," was Madame Koller's reply.

"Hardly that," said Pembroke, quietly. "Made drunk by your precious cousin, Ahlberg."

"I'll send Louis away if you desire me," cried Madame Koller, eagerly.

"I desire nothing of the kind. It is no affair of mine. Come, Cole, you've done the best you could by apologizing. I'll see that those fellows say nothing about it. Good evening, Madame Koller."

"Must you go, Pembroke—now—"

"Immediately. Good-bye," and in two minutes he and Cole were out of the house.

CHAPTER VII.

TO say that Pembroke was angry with Cole is hardly putting it strong enough. He ardently longed that he might once again inflict a thrashing upon him like those Cole had been wont to receive in his school days. He had taken the little clergyman to Malvern, and kept him a day or two before sending him home to his mother. Cole's remorse was pitiful. He wanted to write to the whole House of Bishops, to make a public reparation, to do a number of quixotic things which Pembroke's strong sense forbade peremptorily. When after two days of sincere, but vociferous penitence, Mr. Cole was at last sent back to his rectory, he went under strict instructions from Pembroke to keep his misfortune to himself. But alas for poor Cole! What stung him most was that Madame Koller should have seen him in that condition—for the two hard slaps that she had given him had by no means cured his infatuation. On the contrary, her strong nerves, her fierce temper, her very recklessness of conventionality, irresistibly attracted his timid and conservative nature. What had offended Pembroke, who looked for a certain feminine restraint in all women, and gentleness, even in daring, had charmed Cole. His anguish, when he found, that in addition to his paroxysm of shame, he suffered tortures because he could no longer see Madame Koller, almost frightened him into convulsions.

Pembroke had meant to be very prudent with Ahlberg, and particularly to avoid anything like a dispute. He felt that the natural antagonism between them would be likely to produce a quarrel unless he were remarkably careful, and as he regarded Ahlberg with great contempt, he had a firm determination never to give him either cause or chance of offense. According to the tradition in which he had been raised, a quarrel between two men was liable to but one outcome—an archaic one, it is true, but one which made men extremely cautious and careful not to offend. If a blow once passed it became a tragedy. Pembroke promised himself prudence, knowing that he had not the coolest temper in the world. But when, some days after the dinner, they met, this time in the road also, and Ahlberg's first remark was "What capital fun we had with our friend Cole!" Pembroke's temper instantly got the better of him.

"Mr. Ahlberg, do you think it quite a gentlemanly thing to invite a man like Cole to accept your hospitality in a woman's house, and then deliberately to make him drunk?" asked he.

Ahlberg's sallow skin grew a little paler.

"Is that your view?" he asked, coolly. "I understand something occurred with Madame Koller, which you naturally resent."

As Ahlberg's face grew whiter, Pembroke's grew redder. He felt that first savage impulse to seize Ahlberg and shake him as a mastiff would a terrier. He stood still for a moment or two and then stepping up close to Ahlberg, said to him: "You are a scoundrel."

Ahlberg grew perfectly rigid. This blunt, Anglo-Saxon way of picking a quarrel amazed him. He brought his heels together, and stood up very erect, in the first position of dancing, and said:

"This is most extraordinary. Does Monsieur know that but one result can follow this?"

"Anything you please," answered Pembroke, carelessly, "but if you force me to fight I will certainly kill you. You know something of my pistol practice."

Ahlberg hesitated a moment, and then drawing up his sleeve, exposed a great red knot on his right arm.

"If I desired to take advantage of you I might say that you knew my pistol arm was disabled. I got this six months ago—and it will be six months more before it is well. The paralysis is still partial. But as soon as I can trust it, you will hear from me."

"By all means," answered Pembroke.

Then they touched their hats ceremoniously, and went their way, Pembroke plunging through the brushwood on the side of the road with his dog at his heels.

Pembroke never despised himself more than at that moment. Here was he involved in a quarrel with a man for whom he felt a thorough contempt in every respect, and against which he had particularly warned himself.

As to the method of settling the trouble proposed, that his own good sense condemned, albeit it was still in vogue in Virginia. In the heat of anger he had promised Ahlberg to kill him—while he, Pembroke, knew in his heart, that certainly nothing Ahlberg could say or do, would make him deliberately carry out any such intention. But the folly, wickedness, petulance, want of self-command that brought the quarrel about, enraged him more with himself than with Ahlberg. He could imagine Cave's cool and cutting disapproval—Colonel Berkeley's uproarious and vociferous protest. He knew his own folly in the case so well, that he fancied everybody else must know it too. At all events, the trouble was postponed, and he felt prepared to do a great deal, even to the extent of apologizing to

Ahlberg, rather than fight him. And then Elise. What a creature she was to be sure—singing to him to charm him, and declaiming poetry like the tragic muse—and then that scene with Cole, at which the recollection even made him shudder and laugh too. Why couldn't he fall thoroughly in love with Olivia Berkeley? Probably she would refuse him tartly, but at least it would rid him of Madame Koller, and it would be a bracing, healthy experience. He had half a mind to go back and suggest to Ahlberg that they observe their usual terms toward each other until the time came that Ahlberg might demand satisfaction. A strained demeanor would be peculiarly unpleasant, considering the way the people at The Beeches and the Berkeleys and Miles and himself were associated. But he reflected that Ahlberg was a man of the world, and would probably let things go on smoothly, anyhow. It turned out he was correct, as the next time they met, Ahlberg's manner was imperturbable, and the cold politeness which had always existed between the two men was not visibly changed.

Walking along, and cutting viciously with his stick at the harmless bushes in the path on this particular day, he soon found himself near the fence that ran around the lawn at Isleham. He concluded he would go in and see the Berkeleys for half an hour. It would be a refreshing change from Madame Koller and Ahlberg to Olivia's pure, bright face and the Colonel's jovial, wholesome chaff. It was a mild, spring-like day in early winter. The path led to the lawn through the old-fashioned garden, where everything was brown and sere except the box hedge that stiffly bordered the straight, broad path that led through the garden. He remembered having heard Miles at breakfast say something about going over to Isleham, and was therefore not surprised to see him walking up and down the path with Olivia. She had a book in her hand and was reading in her low, clear voice, aloud to him as they walked slowly, and Miles was following what she read closely, occasionally stopping to ask a question and looking quite cheerful and interested. It came back to him that Miles had spoken of Olivia and himself taking up Italian together. From her manner, and from the expression on her charming face in its little black velvet hood, he saw she was doing it for Miles' sake. He loved that younger brother as well as one human being ever loved another. To have saved the boy one pang he would have done much—but he could do so little! Miles was no longer fit for field sports, society he shunned, reading he could do for himself. Pembroke felt every day the masculine inability to console. Yet here was this girl who had found something to interest poor little Miles, and was doing it with the sweetest womanliness in the world. She probably cared nothing for Italian, but Miles was fond of it.

"Wait," said Olivia, with authority, as he came up. "Don't speak a word. I must let you see how well I can read this," and she read a stanza correctly enough.

"That will do," remarked Pembroke, who knew something of Italian, "you were wise to choose that Francesca da Rimini story though. It is the easiest part in the whole book."

Olivia slammed the volume together indignantly, and drew down her pretty brows in a frown.

"You and papa are always laughing at us. Never mind Miles, *I* don't mind them I assure you."

Pembroke went in and remained to luncheon, as did Miles. The Colonel was in great spirits. He had had a brush on the road with Mrs. Peyton, and had been over to The Beeches.

"And by the way, Pembroke, what's this I hear about poor Cole getting as tight as Bacchus the other night at The Beeches?"

"Nothing at all," answered Pembroke. He did not mean to say anything about Ahlberg's share in it, considering the relations between them, but the Colonel was too sharp for him.

"Now, Cole wouldn't go and do a thing like that unless he was put up to it. Didn't our friend with the waxed mustache have something to do with it, eh? Oh, yes, I see he did."

Pembroke smiled at the way Colonel Berkeley read his face. Olivia spoke up with spirit.

"Papa, I hate that Mr. Ahlberg. Pray don't have him here any more."

But the Colonel looked quite crestfallen at this. Ahlberg amused him, and life was very, very dull for him.

"I hope you won't insist on that, my dear," he said, and Olivia answered:

"I can't when you look that way."

Much relieved, the Colonel began again. "And Madame Koller, I hear—ha! ha!"

"Papa!"

The note of dreadful warning in Olivia's voice vexed Pembroke. But he could not explain and she would not understand.

Afterward, the two brothers walking along briskly toward home, Miles said:

"Do you know I believe Ahlberg is making love to Olivia on the sly!"

Pembroke felt an infinite disgust at this—Ahlberg with his waxed mustache, and his napkin tucked in his waistcoat, and his salmis and his truffles, making love to Olivia Berkeley!

"He doesn't want Madame Koller to know it, though, I'll warrant," continued Miles. "Anybody can see his game there."

"If he asks Olivia to marry him there will be another ear-boxing episode in this neighborhood," said Pembroke with a short laugh.

CHAPTER VIII.

POOR Bob Henry, shut up in the county jail, had indeed said aright when he wrote Pembroke that both blacks and whites were "agin him." Pembroke could scarcely find one of the negro race to testify to Bob Henry's previous good character—and as he sifted his own evidence and surmised the State's, he saw that but for the witness Cave had ferreted out, things would indeed have looked black for Bob Henry. At that time the apprehension as to the way the negroes in their freedom would behave toward the whites was as yet sinister, and the Hibbses, whose relative the dead man was, worked up the feeling against his supposed murderer with considerable astuteness. They were among the largest subscribers to Mr. Cole's salary, and as such they gave their views freely to Mr. Cole upon the impropriety of his going to see Bob Henry in jail, and exerting himself to stem the tide against him among the black people.

Mr. Cole's fair little face flushed up at this criticism delivered from old Mr. Hibbs in a loud and dictatorial voice on the court house green before a crowd of persons.

"Mr. Hibbs—I—I—am a minister of the gospel, sir, and my duty is to condole with the afflicted, sir,—and—however sir,—whatever may be your opinion of that poor wretch in the jail yonder, and however it may conduce to—to—unpopularity, I shall continue to visit him. I have sympathy with the erring," he said, remembering that terrible evening at The Beeches.

A heavy hand descended upon Mr. Cole's shoulder, and Colonel Berkeley's handsome face shone at him.

"Right you are, Cole. You're a little prig sometimes, but you are something of a man, sir—something of a man!"

Mr. Cole blushed with pleasure at this dubious compliment.

Olivia Berkeley's heart was touched with pity for the unfortunate negro. His ailing wife came every day to tell the same rambling and piteous story. Besides, Cave had been at work with her—and he had great power with young imaginations. Pembroke felt a certain anxiety about the case. It was one of those which gave room for the sympathetic oratory which in the country districts in the South yet obtains. He felt at first that if he could make the jury weep, his success as a lawyer would be assured and immediate. But if he failed it would mean long years of toil at his profession to gain that which by a happy inspiration he could win at a single *coup*. He worked hard, and prepared himself—not solely for oratory, because the

Hibbses had not only engaged a formidable array of local talent, but had got one, if not two great men from afar, and the attorney-general himself, to help the state. Pembroke went to Cave despondent and nervous about this.

"It is the best thing in the world for you," answered Cave. "Don't you see, the prosecution has taken the form of a persecution? And the bringing in of outside talent is the greatest luck I ever heard of. The jury, if I know anything of human nature, will not try the prisoner according to the law and the evidence. They will try you and the lawyers from elsewhere—with a strong predisposition in favor of their own county man. It will go hard with them if they can't find some way to discount the outsiders. Of course, I don't say that this feeling will be immediately developed, but it will come out just as certainly as arithmetical progression."

"I hope so," Pembroke answered devoutly.

The day of the trial came—a sunshiny one in midwinter. Every man in the county turned out. Nothing delights a rural Virginian so much as a forensic argument. He will ride twenty miles to hear it, and sit it out, in cold, or heat, or wet, or misery, or anything. Then, besides the interest naturally attaching to the case, was the curiosity to see and hear Pembroke. He had not added to his popularity by his absence after the war—and Madame Koller had been a millstone around his neck latterly. His father and his grandfather and his great-grandfather had been great lawyers before him—indeed there was no tradition or history which went back to the time when there had not been a Pembroke practicing successfully at the bar in the county. So while there was a current of disapproval against him, there was a strong undercurrent of local sympathy in his favor also.

Pembroke appeared early on the ground that morning, with Miles. It was his first opportunity except at the Campdown races to meet the county people of all classes generally. He went about among them cool, affable, and smiling.

"Oyez, oyez, oyez!" the sheriff's loud voice rang out from the court house steps—and the crowd poured into the old brick building, and Pembroke, slipping in by another way entered upon the strain which lasted for five days and nights.

Great as the crowd was at first, it increased every day. Within two hours of the swearing in of the jury, just what Cave had predicted came to pass. The prosecution saw that the jury was on the side of a Pembroke—the Pembrokes had always been prime favorites with juries in that county, and the present one was no exception. Naturally, this nettled the attorney-general and the other great men who appeared for the State. It was certainly an exasperating thing to come so far to find twelve men obstinately bent on seeing things from the point of view of a handsome, plausible young advocate. The court, however, was all that could be desired. The attorney-general expressed his belief to his colleagues that if French Pembroke relied upon an eloquent speech, and the precedent of a Pembroke always carrying the winning colors in a jury trial, he would be mistaken—because Judge Randolph, silent and grim, looked keenly after the law. It was, as Pembroke knew, no easy undertaking to face the array of lawyers before him. Like them, he was shrewd enough to see that it would be a poor triumph to obtain a verdict that would not stand. Bob Henry became to him merely an incident. He looked day after day, during the trial, at the negro's ashy, scared face in the prisoner's dock, and sometimes felt a kind of wonder that a creature so ignorant and so inconsequential could be of such tremendous importance to any human being. For Bob Henry took up Pembroke's mind, his soul, his nights, his days. He worked all day for him, the tension never weakening from the time he entered the court room in the morning, until by the light of sputtering candles he saw Bob Henry walked off in the sheriff's custody at night. Then Pembroke would go to his little office, and lighting his lamp, begin work on his books and his notes. Even Cave and Miles were unwelcome then. He was engaged in a fierce intellectual struggle that he must fight out for himself. He had meant in the beginning to keep himself in condition, but he found out that it was one of the times when the soul triumphs over the body. He would throw himself on the lounge in his office toward daylight and snatch three or four hours of heavy and dreamless sleep, and then wake up with his faculties as keen and tireless as if he had slept for a week. He did not grow haggard and wild-eyed as men sometimes do under these excitements. He was pale, but singularly self-possessed and alert, and looked invariably trim and composed. He forgot everything in those days but the negro he was trying to save from the gallows. The lawyers who opposed him pounded him unmercifully. They too, caught the infection of enthusiasm. It would be scandalous to be beaten by an untried hand in such a case as that, with such admirable fighting ground as they had.

One afternoon, when the court adjourned early on account of a slight illness of one of the jurors, Pembroke mounted his horse and rode off far into the woodlands. When he was out of sight of the village he put spurs to his horse and dashed along the country road. It did him good. He felt already as if he had gained strength enough to last him even at the rate he was using it up if the trial should last two weeks more. Presently he brought his horse down to a walk, and enjoyed the strange restfulness and strength he felt possessing him. Suddenly he came face to face with Olivia Berkeley, riding quietly along the same road.

It would be no exaggeration to say he had forgotten her existence. He had not thought once of her or of Madame Koller, or Ahlberg, anybody but Bob Henry. It had not been ten days since he had seen her, but he felt as if it had been ten years. She looked very pretty and Amazon-like on her light-built black, in her close habit.

"Papa tells me great things of you," she said, after the first greeting. "He is up, storming and swearing for breakfast by sunrise, so as to be at the court-house by nine o'clock. I never expected to see him so happy again in dear old Virginia. It is some excitement for him. As for Jane, she is beginning to think Bob Henry a martyr and a hero combined."

Pembroke smiled. It was not the first praise that had reached his ears, but the first that he had heeded. He had quite lost sight in the last few extraordinary days of any outside view of what he was doing—but praise from a pretty woman—especially praise so obviously sincere, is dear to man's heart.

"I am sorry the Colonel should be so uproarious in consequence of the trial."

"He is, I assure you. But I—I—too, feel very great interest in your success. How much more noble this is than dawdling on the continent! You will not get any money by it, but think—the whole county will admire and applaud you—and think of those two poor black creatures."

"You are crediting me with more than I deserve," he said, finding it difficult to explain that what he was doing had long passed out of the region of a desire for applause, and indeed, of the feeling of compassion which had once inspired him. Now it was the overpowering intellectual and natural bent that was having its own way. Pembroke had been born a lawyer, although he did not suspect it.

In taking his thoughts back to that remote period before the trial begun, Olivia had brought Madame Koller to mind.

"Have you seen Elise—Madame Koller—lately?" The first name slipped out involuntarily. He rarely called Madame Koller by it at any time—but now, by one of those tricks which memory serves all people, her name came to his lips not only without his will, but against it. His face turned a deep red, and he bit his lip in anger and vexation. Olivia straightened herself up on her horse and smiled at him that peculiar indulgent smile, and addressed him in those gentle tones that betokened the freezing up of her sympathies and the coming to life of her contempt. He knew only too well the meaning of that appalling sweetness. "No, I have not. But to-morrow I will probably see her. Shall I remember you to her?"

"If you please," replied Pembroke, wishing Madame Koller at the devil, as he often did. Often—but not always.

Then they drifted into commonplace, and presently they parted, Pembroke galloping back to the village, despising himself almost as much as the day he had allowed his anger to lead him into the quarrel with Ahlberg.

But when he reached his dingy little office, Olivia Berkeley, Madame Koller, Ahlberg, all faded rapidly out of his mind. That great game of skill in which he was engaged, the stake being a human life, again absorbed him. And then the critical time came, when, after having tried to prove that the negro's blow had not killed Hackett, he had to bring out his theory that a dead and missing man was the murderer. Hackett's boon companions, who formed a community of lawless loafers, had been unaccountably shy about attending the trial. Like the rest of their class, they regarded a sensational murder trial as the most fascinating occasion in life. They were great frequenters of the court house, particularly of its low drinking places during "court week," but not one of them showed up in the first days of the trial. Cave brought this significant news to Pembroke, who knew few persons in the miscellaneous crowd that he saw every day. It made his heart beat hard and fast with the hope of a coming success. The Hibbses and their retainers, and a certain set of people who overcame their dislike to the Hibbs family out of exaggerated sympathy for a Northern man with Southern sympathies, for which Hackett had posed, formed a kind of camp to themselves in the court room.

The lawyers for the State found out that Pembroke knew all the weak spots in their theory that Bob Henry's blow killed Hackett, but there was no suspicion of any evidence forthcoming to support Pembroke's theory that another hand struck the blow. Hackett's association with the deserters had evidently been carefully concealed by him, as it would have ostracized him utterly.

Therefore, when Pembroke, putting off until the last possible moment, summoned John Jones and George Robinson and about a dozen others of the "deserters' gang," as it was called, his opponents were taken by surprise. One day only was taken up with their evidence. Each witness, debarred by Judge Randolph's orders from communicating with the other, told a rambling, lying, frightened story, out of which Pembroke gleaned the midnight carousal, a quarrel, a blow—all of them running away, and leaving Hackett to his fate. In one point, however, they all agreed—that the man, William Marsh, who was fearfully cut by Hackett's knife, and who disappeared to die, was the one who struck the fatal blow that knocked Hackett senseless, and from which he never rallied. All were eager to lay it on the dead man, and so to shift the suspicion from themselves. The State, of course, impugned the character of the witnesses, but that was a work of supererogation. They had no characters to impugn. Yet, both judge and jury saw, that without the slightest objection to perjuring themselves on the part of this precious gang, they were involuntarily proving that Marsh, not Bob Henry, was the murderer. Then Cave's protégé, a small, ragged, undersized boy of fifteen, was introduced. He was diffident, and shy, and trembling in every limb, but his testimony was perfectly plain and straightforward, so much so that an eminent gentleman on the side of the prosecution, roared out to him, "Now, young man, tell us if this remarkably straight story of yours didn't have help from somewhere. Have you talked with anybody about this evidence?"

"Y—y—yes, sir," stammered the boy, frightened half out of his life.

"Who was it?" thundered the lawyer.

"Mr.—Mr.—Cave."

"Aha, I thought so. Now, sir, tell us what Mr. Cave said to you—and be careful—very careful."

The boy looked perfectly helpless and hopeless for a moment. Pembroke almost felt himself tremble.

"He said—he said, sir, some of the lawyers would holler at me, and maybe confuse me—but if I jes' stuck to the truth, and didn't tell nothin' but what I seen with my own eyes, I'd come out all right!"

Shouts of applause greeted this, which the sheriff vainly tried to quell. The great man remarked to his personal staff, *sotto voce*, "It's all up. Pembroke's case is too strong for us."

It was late in the afternoon of the fifth day when Pembroke's closing argument was over, and the jury had been instructed and had retired. The Judge's instructions rather damped Pembroke's hopes. The testimony of the deserters, while actually of great effect, was legally not worth much—their motive in shoveling the blame on Marsh was too obvious. And Cave's protégé, although his testimony was remarkably straightforward, was little better than a vagabond boy. Pembroke was not so sanguine of his own success as his opponents were.

The court house was dimly lighted by a few sputtering candles and an ill-burning lamp. The Judge sat up straight and stern, fatigued with the long trial, but willing to wait until six o'clock, the usual hour of adjournment, for the jury. The shabby court-room was filled with men, eager, talkative, but almost breathless with excitement—for by some occult means, they divined that the jury wouldn't be long making up its verdict.

The negro sat in the dock, more ghastly, more ashy than ever. Pembroke rose to go to his office. He felt his iron nerve beginning to give way, but a voice—piteous and pleading—reached him.

"Fur God's sake, Marse French, doan' go 'way. I want you fur ter stay by me."

Pembroke sat down again, this time a little nearer the poor prisoner, whose eyes followed him like a dog's.

A hush settled down upon the audience. There was no pretense of attending to any other business. The opposing lawyers rested wearily in uncomfortable postures about the court-room. They talked in whispers among themselves. Pembroke knew by instinct what they were saying. It was that the jury was hopelessly gone, but that there remained hope yet in the stern and silent Judge, whose instructions had been brief and in no way indicative of which way his judgment inclined. It was not the result of this trial which concerned them, it was the prospect of another.

Among practiced lawyers, nothing is easier to tell than the views of a judge on a criminal case—after the decision has been rendered. About an hour of the suspense had been endured when a message came that the jury had agreed upon a verdict. The expectant crowd suddenly became hushed and motionless. Not as wise as the lawyers, there was utter uncertainty among them as to—not only whether the prisoner was guilty or not, but whether Pembroke alone and single-handed, had vanquished the veterans before him.

The jury filed in and took their places, and the formalities were gone through, when the foreman said in a loud voice, "Not guilty." A wild and tumultuous cheering broke forth. Like the poor prisoner, Pembroke felt dazed. The end was not yet by any means. The opposing lawyers were on their feet in a moment—the sheriff shouted for order—and in the midst of this, a sudden silence came and Pembroke found himself—he hardly knew how—on the platform shaking hands with Judge Randolph.

"I congratulate you, sir," he heard the Judge's voice saying afar off. "You have maintained the reputation of your distinguished father for the tact and judgment with which you have defended your client. You have a great career before you. It is most encouraging to see such an example among the younger members of the bar."

Then there was a wild commotion. Pembroke felt himself choking, trembling, utterly unable to reply. The pause to hear what he would say became painfully prolonged. He began "Your Honor"—and after repeating it twice, became utterly dumb.

"You may retire, Mr. Pembroke," said Judge Randolph, with a smile, "your modesty is equal to your abilities."

At this Pembroke felt himself seized by the legs. The crowd carried him out into the night air where another crowd yelled and shouted, he struggling and breathless, and presenting a more undignified appearance than he had ever imagined himself capable of looking. The next thing he found himself on the court-house steps. While in the din and confusion, he recognized occasionally faces by the light of the swinging lantern in the porch of the building. In a moment the attorney-general of the State appeared by his side—a handsome florid man of sixty. He waved imperiously for silence, and the crowd obeyed.

"My friends," he said, in a strong, musical voice, "our young friend here has made a magnificent fight." (Yells and cheers.) "He has done more than make an eloquent speech. He has mastered the law in the case." (More yells and shouts.) "It was the intention of my colleagues and myself to move for a new trial. We have abandoned that intention." (Yells and shouts wilder and wilder.) "We might possibly get a new trial on technicalities. It would cost the county much, and it would not subserve the cause of justice—for I cheerfully acknowledge to you here, that our young friend has proved conclusively that whoever caused the death of the dead man, the prisoner did not. Now will you not unite with me in giving him three cheers and a tiger!"

The uproar was terrific. Pembroke could say nothing, could do nothing, but bow. Suddenly an inspiration came to him. He turned to the attorney-general who stood behind him and shook hands with him warmly. The other lawyers crowded around him and shook hands. Somebody made way through the crowd for Bob Henry. The negro on seeing Pembroke broke into loud sobbing, and seizing him in both arms called down blessings on him. Then Colonel Berkeley shouldered his way up to him with Miles. At every minute the enthusiasm of the crowd increased. Pembroke was growing deadly pale. The excitement, the sleeplessness, of the last week was telling on him at last. Colonel Berkeley, after a sharp glance at him, took him by the arm, and by dint of hauling and pulling succeeded in wedging his way with Pembroke through the crowd, which in the hullaballoo and semi-darkness, did not know that the hero of the hour was gone, and yelled fiercely, "Speech! Speech!" The attorney-general gratified them.

Colonel Berkeley hustled Pembroke down, back through the court-room, out of a side door, and through byways to where the Isleham carriage stood, and clapped him in it, jumping in after him.

"Cave will look after Miles," he said, and shouted to Petrarch, who was on the box, "Home." The coachman laid the whip on his horses and they made the five miles to Isleham in half an hour.

When they reached the house, everything was too recent with Pembroke—his final speech, the excitement, the relief, the collapse—for him to have recovered himself. Olivia met them in the hall. Her father, who relished a new sensation as only a man who loves sensations can, was joyous.

"Congratulate him, my love," he called out in his merry, jovial voice. "He is a true son of old French Pembroke. Great Cæsar! Haven't I seen your father carry everything before him just like this! Would that he were alive this night! My darling, you should have heard his speech—a regular Burr and Blennerhassett speech, Olivia—and the effect—by Jove, my dear, I can't describe it—and the Judge called him up on the bench to congratulate him—and—and—"

The Colonel surged on, telling everything at once. Olivia listened with shining eyes. She had held out her hand to Pembroke in the beginning, and as her father talked she continued to hold the hand in her little strong clasp. For the first time Pembroke was burnt by the fire in her eyes. What a woman for a man full of ambition to have! He had seen Elise Koller wildly enthusiastic about herself—but Olivia had forgotten all about herself. She was coloring, smiling, and sympathetic about him.

"How glad I am—how splendid of you—for that poor negro, too. God will reward you," she said.

"Now, my boy," cried the Colonel, "What do you want? Your dinner or your bed?"

"My bed," answered Pembroke, smiling, but ready to drop. "I want nothing but sleep, and I want to sleep a week. Thank you, Olivia."

He had never called her by her name since they were boy and girl together. The Colonel in his excitement did not notice it, but Olivia turned a beautiful rosy red. The Colonel dragged Pembroke off to his room. Petrarch put him to bed. Before he slept though, his thoughts returned to Olivia's soft eyes—while Colonel Berkeley, walking the drawing-room floor downstairs, retailed in flamboyant language, to Olivia, the triumphs of the day.

CHAPTER IX.

It took two or three days for Pembroke to recover from his fatigue and excitement. Perhaps he did not hasten his complete recuperation. It was surely pleasanter to come down to a twelve o'clock breakfast, served piping hot by Petrarch, with Olivia to pour his coffee for him, with that morning freshness which is so becoming to a woman, than the loneliness of Malvern, with poor Miles' sad face and pathetic effort to forget himself and the wreck of his boyish life. Cave had taken the boy to his cabin in the pine woods to stay some days, so that there was nothing to call Pembroke back home. Miles was happier than for a long time. Cave spoke to him with a certain bracing encouragement that Olivia's pitiful sympathy and his brother's sharp distress lacked. There was more of the salt of common sense in what Cave said than in Olivia's unspoken consolation, which much as it charmed the boy, sometimes left him sadder than it found him. She was so sorry for him that she could not always disguise it.

So a few days went on, and Pembroke began to find Olivia every hour pleasanter, more winning—until one night in his own room, after Olivia had played to him half the evening and had read to him the other half, he took himself to task. In the first place, he did not want to marry at all then. He had a great many things to do first. Then, there was a serious obstacle in the way, even had all the rest been smoothed out. The Pembroke fortune, such as it was, was on its last legs. With the negroes gone, and the land frightfully reduced in value, there was only a slender competence left—and those two years in Paris had cost a pretty penny. Only during the last few weeks Pembroke had waked up to the true condition of affairs. Miles must be provided for, and upon a scale more suited to Pembroke's tastes than his resources. Then, there remained for the elder brother, nothing. He had not thought of this when he borrowed money at a high interest so merrily while he was in Paris—but as he was every day awaking to his manlier self, this had come home to him in its true light. He was not a man to ask any woman to share poverty with him. To have brought a woman down, as his wife, from a state of former luxury, would have been a misery too keen. Rather would he have died—for false as well as true pride had great share in him. Therefore, he thought, as he sat in his room smoking, it would be better that he did not get his wings scorched. It was to his credit that he did not allow any supposition that Olivia cared for him to enter into his calculation.

"Sweet Olivia," he thought to himself, "some luckier man will win you. I shall be ten years too late,"—and then he sighed, and presently began to whistle cheerfully. But one thing was sure. He would never marry Elise Koller. Even though his eyes were opened now to the fact that he was virtually a ruined man, there was no longer any chance that the baser part of him would succumb to that temptation.

It was pleasant—especially the Colonel's jolly company, to say nothing of Petrarch's, who highly approved of Pembroke, and remarked as he industriously brushed his clothes on the last night, "I clar, Marse French, you sutny do favor yo' par. I 'member de time he made that argyument when Marse Jack Thornton, he mos' kilt Marse Spott Randolph on 'count o' Miss Tilly Corbin. We had ole wuks dat time. 'Twuz when me an' Marse was co'tin' missis. I tell yo' par, 'A eye fur a eye,' 'a toof fur a toof, an' I will resist de cripplers, say de Lord.' Marster an' me went to de cote house ter hear him. I tho't 'bout it de yether night, when de white folks was a crowdin' 'roun' an' shakin' yo' han' an' clappin' you on de back. Arter you went up st'yars, Miss Livy, she come an' say to me, 'Petrarch, did you hear de speech?' I say, 'Lord, honey, dat I did. You jes' oughter seen de folks whoopin' an' hollerin' and Marse French he stannin' up, lookin' handsome like he mar'—you aint forgit yo' mar, has you, Marse French?"

"No," said Pembroke.

"I reklecks her when she warn't no older 'n Miss Livy. She was kinder light on her feet like Miss Livy, and she had dem shinin' eyes, an dat ar way Miss Livy got o' larfin' at yer. She an' mistis' was mighty good frien's, jes' like you par an' marse, an' David an' Jonadab. Dey use ter come here an' stay a week—yo' mar come in de kerridge wid Miss 'Lizbeth an' Marse Miles, an' yaller Betsy—she was a likely nigger, but a dretful sinner,—an' you on a little pony ridin' by yo' par's side. Lordy how you did useter tease Miss Livy an' dem chillen! Some times you mek Miss Livy cry—an' cry, an' de tears wuz like de waters o' Babylon."

"What a brute I must have been! Why didn't you or yellow Betsy get me a lathering?"

"Hi, Marse French, boys is boys. Dey c'yarn help bein' troublesome an' dirty an' teasin'. Gord done made 'em so. 'My people is rambunctious,' He say, an' I ain't never seen no boys 'cept what was dirty an' tormentin'."

At last, Pembroke felt he had no excuse for remaining longer at Isleham, and besides, he was seriously afraid of falling in love with Olivia. So he took his way back to Malvern.

While at Isleham, he had got one or two cocked-hatted notes from Madame Koller. But on reaching home he found that one arrived with great regularity every morning and occasionally during the day beside. The tenor of all was the same. Why did he not come to see his friend. She was so lonely. The country was *triste* at best. Pembroke felt very like asking her if the country was so triste then why did she not go away. But he was a gentleman as well as a man, and was patient with women even in their follies.

At last, when he could put it off no longer—as indeed he had no tangible reason for not going to see Madame Koller—he went. She received him in her little sitting-room, adapting at the time one of her prettiest poses for his benefit. She had heard of his triumph and was full of pretty congratulations—but in some way, she could not strike the note of praise that would harmonize. She didn't know anything about professional men. She had lived in Europe long enough to get the notion that it was rather vulgar to work for pay—not that Pembroke got any pay in this case. But if Pembroke had married her, that weather-beaten sign "Attorney-at-Law" would have come down from his office in the village, and the office itself would have lost its tenant—so she thought.

Pembroke always felt a delicacy in asking her to sing, but Madame Koller often volunteered to do it, knowing Pembroke's passionate fondness for music, and feeling that truly on that ground they were in sympathy. Olivia Berkeley's finished and charming playing pleased and soothed him, but it was nothing to the deep delight that Madame Koller's music gave him—for when she sat down to the piano and playing her own accompaniments sang to him in her fervid way, it simply enchanted him—and Madame Koller knew it. Although he was exasperatingly cool under the whole battery of her smiles and glances, yet when she sang to him, he abandoned himself to the magic of a voice.

While she seated herself at the piano and began to sing, Pembroke, stretched out in a vast chair, glanced sidewise at her. She did not mouth and grimace in singing as many women do. She opened her wide, handsome mouth, and seemed only to be calmly smiling, while her voice soared like a bird. She had, in short, no amateurish tricks.

Her profile, with its masses of yellow hair, was imposing. She was no mere slip of a girl. When she had sung to him for the best part of an hour she thought the time had come for her reward. So she went back to her place on the sofa near the fire and posed beautifully. Pembroke almost groaned. The singing was delicious enough, but the sentimental hair-splitting had long since palled—and besides, the lady was too much in earnest.

"You remained several days, did you not, at the Colonel's?"

"Yes," said Pembroke, cheerfully, and thinking gloomily how very like a matrimonial lecture was the ensuing conversation. These interviews with

Madame Koller always disinclined him extremely to giving any woman the power to ask him searching questions. Only, he did not believe Olivia Berkeley was an inquisitive woman—she was quite clever enough to find out what she wished to know without asking questions.

The only remark Madame Koller made in reply was, "Ah,"—and lapsed into silence, but the silence did not last long.

"Olivia must have been very charming."

"Immensely," answered Pembroke, with much heartiness, and wishing Madame Koller would sing again. He hardly knew which was the more exasperating, Madame Koller's tone to him in speaking of Olivia, or Olivia's tone in speaking of Madame Koller.

"Olivia is so excessively tame," said she, after a pause. "So cold—so self-contained."

"I don't think she lacks spirit, though," responded Pembroke, with the easy air of a man discussing the most trivial subject, although he swore mentally at Madame Koller for introducing the subject. "Miss Berkeley has the reticence of a gentlewoman. But by heaven! I wouldn't like to arouse that spirit of hers."

Madame Koller sighed. It was a real and genuine sigh. She was thinking how hard and strange it was that she was not permitted by fate to be either a complete gentlewoman or a complete artist. She had learned in her student days, and in that brief and brilliant artistic period, to be reticent about her money matters, but that was all. She saw even in her Aunt Sally Peyton, whom she regarded as an interfering old person, without any style whatever, a certain air of security in what she said and did—a calm indifference to her world—that Madame Koller was keen enough to know marked the gentlewoman—which she, Elise Koller, who had ten times the advantages, and had twenty times the knowledge of the world that old Mrs. Peyton had, was never quite sure—there just was a little uncertainty—ah, it was very little, but it made a great deal of difference.

"America seems queer enough to me now," she said presently.

"Very likely," answered Pembroke. "You have remained here much longer already than I expected."

Madame Koller at this fixed her eyes upon Pembroke in a way that made him wince. A blush, too, showed through his dark skin.

"Can you—can you—say *that* to me?" she cried.

Like any other man under the same circumstances, Pembroke remained perfectly silent—because it is a well-known fact that when a woman takes the initiative in tender speeches, the man, if he be a man, is at once silenced. But Madame Koller was fluent.

"I know what you think of me," she said. This surprised Pembroke, who really did not know what he thought of her. "You think me the weakest woman in the world. But I have been strong. While my husband lived, heaven knows what I endured. He was the cruelest creature God ever made."

Pembroke thought it was the same old story of continental husbands and wives. He had once known a marchese who made no secret that he occasionally beat his marchesa. But Madame Koller almost made him smile at the grotesqueness of what she told him, although it was real enough to her to make her weep in the telling.

"He was always ill—or imagining himself ill. He took medicine until he nearly drove me crazy with his bottles and plasters. He lived in a bath chair when he was as well able to walk about as I was—and I was chained to that bath chair. Everything made him ill—even my singing. He would not let me sing—only think of it—think of it."

Madame Koller glanced at Pembroke through her tears. He had stood up and was saying something vague but comforting. The late Mr. Koller was indeed a dreadful reminiscence.

"Banish that time as far as you can," he said. "The present is yours."

"Is it?" she said. "Now I will say to you that black as that past is, it is not so black as this present. Now I endure torments far greater than any I felt then."

Pembroke's strong jaw was set resolutely. He felt rising tumultuously within him that masculine pity that has wrecked many men. He would not, if he could help it, prove false to himself with this woman, in spite of her tears and her voice.

"What have you to say to me?" she demanded, after a pause.

"This," answered Pembroke, with much outward boldness. "That your coming here is an unsuccessful experiment. The same things that made this country life distasteful to you in your childhood even, make it distasteful now. This is not your native atmosphere. You will never be anything but morbid and wretched here. This country life is like death to you—and almost like death to me."

"Then why—why—"

"Why do I stand it? Because I must. Because as a man, I must. Here is my work, my duty, my manhood. Don't be surprised to hear me talk this way. You haven't heard me speak of these things before—but still they govern me some—more of late than they used to do. There is a good deal here that is melancholy enough to me—but I would be a poltroon if I started out to make life amusing. You see, I have considerable ambition—and that impels me to work."

Madame Koller surveyed him keenly. By degrees the fire of resentment rose in her eyes. She was angered at his coolness, at his calm reasoning. Prudence in love is commonly regarded as a beggarly virtue by women.

"After all," she said, "what are you to me? Nothing but a whim, a caprice. But had you spoken to me a year ago as you do now, I should not be here."

Pembroke remembered with a blush some slight love-making episodes, and her tone stung him.

"I can play the rascal if you like," he said, angrily. "I can pretend to feel what I don't feel, but I warn you, I shan't be a pleasant rascal. If ever I take to villainy I shall probably take to drink and gambling too."

Madame Koller sat down discontentedly on the sofa. When Pembroke had arrived that afternoon her intention had been to determine one thing or another—for life at The Beeches could not be endured much longer. It mattered little what old Madame Schmidt said, but her cousin, Ahlberg, was getting restive and threatened to leave her—and she was mortally afraid of being left in America alone. But what progress had she made? None. And suppose Pembroke were to leave that house her lover, would it not be the greatest act of folly she had ever committed?—and she had had her follies. And so she was tossed hither and thither by prudence and feeling, and condemning her own weakness, yet tamely submitted to it.

Meanwhile, Pembroke had decided for himself. This thing could go on no longer. He felt at that moment as if he had had enough of love-making to last him for the next ten years. And besides, he had withstood enough to make him feel that he did not care to withstand any more. So he picked up his hat with an air of great determination.

"I must leave you," he said. "Elise, you have given me many happy hours, but it would be ruin for us to become either more or less than friends."

Madame Koller had thought herself thoroughly prepared for this, which her own sense told her was literally true. But suddenly, without a moment's warning, without her own volition, and almost without her knowledge, she burst into violent weeping. Was it for this she had come the interminable distance—that she had suffered horrors of loneliness and ennui? Alas, for her!

Pembroke was appalled. Apparently all was to do over again, but there was no longer any room for weakness. His mind was made up and could not be unmade. He only stood silent, therefore, biting his lip, while his face grew crimson.

For the first time in his life he hailed Ahlberg as a relief—for at that moment Ahlberg appeared on the threshold. Madame Koller pulled herself together as quickly as she had given way.

"Ah, Louis, you are welcome. Do not go yet," to Pembroke.

Pembroke did not take the hint. He went immediately.

CHAPTER X.

THE sudden pang which wrenched poor Mr. Cole's heart when he heard that Madame Koller would soon leave the county, and the country as well, was vain suffering. For Madame Koller did not go. Old Madame Schmidt for the first time became restless. Ahlberg protested that he could not stay any longer. Pembroke had become entirely at ease about Ahlberg. Apparently Ahlberg was in no hurry to carry out that rash engagement to fight, which Pembroke regarded on his own part as a piece of consummate folly, and was heartily ashamed of. He did not feel the slightest apprehension that, if the truth got out, his personal courage would be suspected, because that had been tested during the war, but he was perfectly willing to let Ahlberg's arm take as long to recover as it chose, and called himself a fool every time he thought about the roadside quarrel.

The ennui was nearly killing to Madame Koller, yet she stayed on under a variety of pretexts which deceived everybody, including herself.

She was not well adapted for solitude, yet most of the people about bored her. Mrs. Peyton, she considered as her bête noir, and quite hated to see the Peyton family carriage turning into the carriage drive before the door. But for her singing she would have died. But just as long as the wheezy old grand piano in the drawing-room would hold together, she would not be quite friendless. Pembroke had not been to see her since that afternoon when she had wept so. But she conveyed to him one day when she met him at Isleham, that he need not be afraid to come to see her. Man like, Pembroke could not resist this challenge, and went—and found Madame Koller received him more like an ordinary visitor than ever before. Consequently he went again. Another motive which impelled him was the talk that would arise in the county if he ceased going to The Beeches at all. Everybody would imagine there had been a breach, and if a breach, a former friendship.

Cave, one day, met Madame Koller at Isleham. When she told him of her loneliness he was stricken with pity for not having been to see her. Like Colonel Berkeley, he thought her presence in Virginia was explained by money troubles, and asked permission to visit her mother and herself, Madame Schmidt being invariably brought in by Madame Koller as if she were a real person instead of a mere breathing automaton. And so he went.

"What a strange, fascinating man is your friend Cave," she said afterward to Pembroke upon one of his occasional formal visits, when their conversation was always upon perfectly safe and general subjects.

"I never discovered any strange fascination about him," laughed Pembroke with masculine practicality.

"He lives in the woods. Yet he understands art better than any man I know."

"There's nothing extraordinary. He is a highly educated man. The doctors tell him he can't live except in the pine woods, but his two rooms in his log cabin are more comfortable than any I have at Malvern."

"By the way, you have never invited me to Malvern. I used to go there as a girl."

Pembroke remembered a speech of his friend's, Mrs. Peyton, to him some time before.

"Ah, my dear French," she had said, "what a dear, sweet, amiable creature your mother was—and your father was a regular Trojan when he was roused. I remember taking Eliza there for a visit once, when she was growing up, and the singing mania had just possessed her. She sung all day and nearly all night—screech, screech—bang, bang on the piano. Your father almost danced, he was so mad—but your dear mother was all thoughtfulness. 'My dear Sally,' she would say every day laughing. 'Don't feel badly about Eliza's singing, and the way Mr. Pembroke takes it. It is the only chance John Cave has to say a word to Elizabeth.' Your mother was highly in favor of that match, I can tell you, though John had no great fortune—and your father was so fond of him too, that he really imagined John was courting him, instead of Elizabeth. But I shortened my visit considerably, I assure you."

All this flashed through Pembroke's mind when Madame Koller spoke. And then he colored slightly. He was a little ashamed of the dilapidation of a once fine country house. During the war, the place had been raided and the house fired. The fire had been quickly extinguished, but the front porch and a part of one wing was charred. He felt some false, though natural shame at this, particularly as Ahlberg, when he and Pembroke were on visiting terms, had never been to the place without intimating that it was queer they did not have the house thoroughly rehabilitated. But Pembroke had inherited a soul of Arab hospitality, and he answered promptly:

"Whenever you and Madame Schmidt will honor me with a visit, you will be most welcome."

"And will you ask Mr. Cave, too?"

"Certainly. Mr. Cave is my closest friend."

Just as on a similar occasion, Colonel Berkeley had incurred Olivia's wrath by inviting the Pembrokes to meet Madame Koller, so Miles, meaning to do the most agreeable thing in the world, informed Pembroke a day or two after he had mentioned that Madame Koller and her mother and Cave were coming to luncheon on Tuesday, that meeting Colonel Berkeley, he, Miles, had invited the Colonel and Olivia over for Tuesday, also—to meet the others. Miles walked away, whistling to his dog, serenely unconscious of the chagrin that overwhelmed Pembroke at this apparently harmless information.

Pembroke did not swear, although he was profane upon occasions—but when Aunt Keturah, his old nurse and housekeeper, came to him the next minute to ask something about the proposed festivity, his answer was,

"Go to the devil!"

Aunt Keturah was naturally offended at this.

"I didn't never think *my* mistis' son gwin' talk dat discontemptuous way to de mammy dat nuss him and Miss 'Lizbeth, and Marse Miles, an' lay yo' par out, and your mar, an' set by Miss 'Lizbeth an' hole her han' 'twell de bref lef' her body—" For your true African never omits to mention any family tragedy or sorrow or other lugubrious proceedings in which he or she may have had a part.

"Well, old lady, I didn't exactly mean what I said—"

"Well, den, you hadn't orter said nuttin' like it—"

"I know it. If you were to go to the devil, I don't know what would become of me."

"Dat's so, honey. An' ain't no wife gwi' do fur you like yo' po' ole mammy"—for the possibility of Pembroke's marriage was extremely distasteful to Keturah, as portending her downfall and surrender of the keys.

Colonel Berkeley had often been to Malvern since his return, but Olivia, not since she was a child, when she would go over with her mother, and played in the garden with Miles. Then Pembroke was a tall, overbearing boy, a remorseless tease, whose only redeeming trait, in her childish eyes, was the wonderful stories he could tell out of books—when he chose. Elizabeth she remembered—a beautiful, haughty girl, who alternately snubbed and petted her. It seemed so long ago. They were to come to luncheon at two o'clock. When Olivia and her father drove up, with Cave in the carriage with them, whom they had picked up on the road, Pembroke had been called off for a moment by a client who was interviewing him in "the office"—that necessary adjunct of every professional man, and most of the gentry in Virginia, a comfortable one or two-roomed building, a little back of the "great house," where the master kept his books and accounts, his guns and hunting paraphernalia, where his dogs had the right of entry and his women kind had not.

The house had once been imposing. Two wings rambled off from the center building. One was overgrown with ivy, and looked both comfortable and picturesque under the tall and branching elms. The other was gaunt and scorched and weather-beaten. The heat had cracked the windows and had forced the bricks out of place. One pillar of the porch on that side was gone. The damage to the house was really not great, but apparently it was ruined.

Miles met them at the door—Miles, once the handsome scapegrace, and now the blighted, the unfortunate. The spectacle of his marred face was in melancholy keeping with what surrounded him.

He was genuinely glad to see them. He came down the steps, and gallantly and even with a certain grace, offered Olivia his one arm to alight from the carriage. The Colonel scrambled out and immediately seized Miles.

"My dear fellow, driving through this plantation to-day brought back to me your father's purchase of that woodland down by the creek in 'forty-six."

Anything that occurred in 'forty-six had such a charm for Colonel Berkeley that Miles knew he was in for it. The Colonel took his arm and trotted up and down the portico, pointing out various ways in which the late Mr. Pembroke, his devoted friend, had neglected the Colonel's advice in regard to farming, and the numberless evils that had resulted therefrom. Colonel Berkeley entirely forgot that his own farming was not above reproach, and if he had been reduced to his land for a living, instead of that lucky property at the North that he had so strenuously tried to make way with, he would indeed have been in a bad way. But the Colonel was a famous farmer on paper, was president of the Farmers' Club of the county, had published several pamphlets on subsoil drainage, and was a frequent contributor to the columns of the Southern Planter before the war.

Cave and Olivia, finding themselves temporarily thrown on each other, concluded to walk through the grounds. Madame Koller and her mother had not yet arrived, and under the huge trees, a little distance off, they could see Pembroke talking with his visitor, as the latter mounted his horse to ride away.

In former days the grounds, like the house, had been fine, but now they were completely overgrown and neglected, yet, there was a kind of beauty in their very wildness.

"How charming this wilderness of roses will be when they are in bloom," said Olivia, as they walked through what had once been a rose walk, stiff and prim, now rioting in lush luxuriance. "I remember it quite straight, and the rose trees trimmed up all in exactly the same shape—and see, the roses have climbed so over the arbor that we can't get in."

Cave said nothing. The one love of his life was born and lived and died in this home. He could see, through a rift in the trees, the brick wall around the burying ground where Elizabeth lay. It was fallen away in many places, and the sheep browsed peacefully over the mounds. The marble slab over Elizabeth was as yet new and white. Still Olivia did not jar on him at that moment. She was innately sympathetic.

They paced slowly about the graveled paths overgrown in many places with weeds, and among a vigorous growth of young shrubbery, unpruned and unclipped. She pulled a great branch of pink dogwood from a transplanted forest tree, and swayed it thoughtfully as she walked. Presently they saw Pembroke coming to look for them. As he approached and took Olivia's hand, a color as delicate as that of the dogwood blossoms she held in her other hand, mounted to her face.

Then they turned back leisurely toward the house. At one spot, under a great linden tree, was the basin of a fountain, all yellow and choked with the trailing arbutus, which grew with the wild profusion that marks it in the depth of the woods. The fountain was long since gone. Pembroke plucked some of the arbutus and handed it to Olivia, taking from her the dogwood branch at the same time and throwing it away.

"The arbutus has a perfume—the dogwood has none—and a flower without perfume is like a woman without sentiment," he said gayly. As they stood still for a moment, Olivia suddenly exclaimed to Pembroke:

"Oh, I remember something about this fountain—don't you?" Then they both began to laugh.

"What is it?" asked Cave.

"I was staying here once with mamma, when I was a little girl—"

"I picked you up and held you over the basin to scare you."

"And dropped me in, and—"

"Went gallantly to the rescue and dragged you out—"

"And your mother sent you to bed without your dinner."

"I remember thinking you were the most comical looking object I ever saw with your curls dripping, and I was particularly amused at the chattering of your teeth. What remorseless wretches boys are!"

"I don't believe you meant to let me slip."

"You were splashing in the basin before I knew it. But it seemed a delicious piece of mischief then, and Miles' terror that his turn would come next—Elizabeth boxed my ears for it."

For the first time since their return home each came back to something like the old boy and girl frankness, and they laughed like children.

"How I loved to come here when I was a little girl. Your mother was certainly the most delightful companion for a child. I remember how she allowed me to brush her hair, it was so long and beautiful. I suppose my efforts were torture to her; how splendid she looked when she was dressed for a ball."

Pembroke was touched to the heart. His mother who died like Elizabeth, in her youth and beauty, was only seventeen years older than himself. He remembered that she had been a little more than a girl when he, her eldest son, reached up to her shoulder. Olivia and her father were always associated with his mother. Few persons remembered her, he thought bitterly. He had imagined that it was impossible for any one to know her without being inspired with the profound admiration he felt, along with his affection for her. But naturally it was not so—and he felt an inexpressible pride in hearing Olivia's words. They were not many, but he knew they came from her heart.

"Do you know," he said as they turned away and pursued the path to the house while Cave dropped behind, "I think you are a little like my mother. Petrarch says so too, and Petrarch is a physiognomist."

"Nonsense," cried Olivia, nevertheless coloring with pleasure. "Your mother was one of the most beautiful women in the world, and most commanding in her beauty. I don't know anybody at all like her."

They were now near the house, and looking up, Pembroke saw Madame Koller and the bundle of wrappings she called mamma descending from the carriage. A little unpleasant shock came upon him. The ladies from The Beeches were out of harmony just then.

Nevertheless they were very cordially greeted. Although the day was spring-like, Madame Koller's gown was trimmed with fur, and she cowered close to the fire in the big, draughty drawing-room. Pembroke fancied that

Madame Schmidt's fondness for wrappings would eventually descend to her daughter. But Madame Koller was very handsome. The quiet winter, the country air had made her much younger and fresher. And then, most women are much better looking when they are in love. They live in a perpetual agitation, which gives a strange brightness to the eye, a softness to the smile. They are impelled toward their natural rôle, which is acting. Madame Koller had the benefit of all this.

The luncheon passed off very well. In the house was that queer mixture of shabbiness and splendor common in Virginia country houses. At table they sat in common Windsor chairs, but ate off Sèvres china; a rickety sideboard was loaded down with plate. The Virginians were, as a rule, indifferent to comforts, but luxuries they must have. After the luncheon Pembroke took them to the library, and through such of the house as was habitable. Madame Koller raved over the fine editions of books, the old mahogany furniture, the antique portraits intermingled with daubs of later ancestors—the whole an epitome of the careless pleasure-loving, disjointed life of the dead and gone Virginia—when the people stocked their cellars with the best wines and slept on husk mattresses—where the most elaborate etiquette was maintained in the midst of incongruities of living most startling. It had never ceased to be puzzling to Madame Koller. She admired, as well she might, a lovely girlish portrait of Pembroke's mother which hung in the drawing-room. There was a piteous likeness between it and the one unscarred side of Miles' face.

Miles had kept close to Olivia—he was not quite easy with Madame Koller. As for Madame Schmidt, he had in vain tried to get something out of her, but the old lady was obviously so much more comfortable seated by the drawing-room fire, well wrapped up, with her feet on the footstool, and nobody to distract her attention from keeping warm, that she was considerately left to herself.

But Madame Koller did not enjoy the day, as, indeed, she did not at that phase of her existence enjoy anything. She had fancied she could conquer her heart, in the presence of its object, and with a dangerous rival in the foreground. Love finds a mighty helper in self-love. Whatever determination she might once have had to relinquish Pembroke melted away when she saw that Olivia Berkeley and he were quietly slipping into a state of feeling that would turn to something stronger in a moment of time. And naturally she thought no woman alive could withstand the man that had conquered her.

It was late in the afternoon when the carriages drove off. Olivia said truly she had had a very happy day. Not so truly said Madame Koller.

CHAPTER XI.

THE winter had lapsed into spring. It was April—the May of colder climates. In a week—a day—Nature had rushed into bloom. Even Madame Koller, who cared little for these things, was awakened to the beauty surrounding her. She spent hours walking in the fresh morning air and thinking—thinking. The few times she saw Pembroke, and the quiet, formal courtesy with which he treated her was as wind to flame. In his absence she was perpetually thinking of him, devising wild and extravagant methods of winning him. It was her pride, she now persuaded herself, that needed to be avenged. Again throwing prudence wildly aside, she boldly acknowledged to herself that it was love. For the first time in her life she was thrown upon herself—and a very dangerous and undisciplined self it was. Sometimes she blamed him less than he deserved for whatever folly he had been a party to—and again she blamed him more. Madame Koller was fast working herself up to the point of an explosion.

Toward dusk one evening, as Olivia Berkeley sat in the dim drawing-room where a little fire crackled on the hearth, although the windows were opened to the purple twilight outside, she heard a light step upon the portico—and the next moment, Madame Koller walked in.

Olivia received a kind of shock when she recognized her. Madame Koller's manner to her had been queer of late, but she spoke to her very cordially. Very likely she was wearied and ennuyéd at home—and had to come to Olivia in the desperation of loneliness.

Madame Koller, in response to Olivia's hospitable offer, allowed her to remove the long furred mantle, and place it on a chair. She looked at Olivia fixedly. Her eyes were large and very bright.

"You are surprised that I should come here at this time, Miss Berkeley?"

"I am very pleased, Madame Koller."

"You are surprised. However, is it not strange how in moments of great agitation, trifles will come to one's mind? It reminds me even now, how all the people in this county are amazed at simple—very simple things. There is nothing in my walking a mile or two to see you—I have a servant outside—but you, like the rest, regard it as very queer."

"As you please, Madame Koller," answered Olivia.

"Still more strange will you think it when I tell you my errand—for, although you are no fool, Olivia Berkeley, you have no heart."

"Did you take so much trouble in order to tell me this to-night?" answered Olivia pleasantly enough, but with that little shade of sarcasm in her voice that is infuriating to people in deadly earnest.

"Not entirely. But I am glad you have no heart to suffer. I would not wish any one to suffer as I do."

Madame Koller paused a moment.

"You know why I suffer. It is not my purpose to say how much Pembroke is to blame. I do not know how you cold, self-contained people consider these things. He did not take the trouble to undeceive me, when I supposed he loved me until a few months ago—until you, in short, appeared."

"Madame Koller," said Olivia, haughtily, "may I beg that you will not bring my name into your personal affairs or Pembroke's either? While I am under no obligation to tell you, I have no hesitation in saying that there is nothing whatever between him and me that the whole world may not know. He is not my lover and never has been."

Madame Koller looked at Olivia and laughed mirthlessly.

"You sit there and tell me that as coolly as if you expected me to go home without saying another word. But I will not go, and I will speak. However, there is nothing that you need be angry about. Only this. Pembroke, you see, is poor. He has great gifts, but they will not bring him money for many years. He is extravagant—he is proud. He wants to go into public life—that he has told me. Imagine the terrible future of poverty and debt before him if he marries without a fortune. I can save him from all this. I am rich enough for both. Say that you will not stand in my way. I will remove the only obstacle in his path. I will give up everything. I will stay in this tedious land for his sake. He shall pursue any career he chooses. Think well what it is to rob such a man of his only chance of fortune and ease. For if he does not marry me, he will certainly marry you."

Olivia sat upright in her chair completely dazed. She forgot to be indignant. For the first time the truth enunciated by Madame Koller came home to her. Pembroke *was* poor. He *was* extravagant. He *was* bent upon entering politics. Olivia had, as most women, a practical sympathy. She knew very well the horrors of poverty for such a man, and her portion would be but small.

Madame Koller, seeing that she had made her impression, waited—and after a while continued. Her voice was low and very sweet. She seemed pleading for Pembroke's salvation.

"Pembroke, you know, is already deeply in debt. He cannot readily accommodate himself to the style of provincial living here. He would say all these things are trifles. I tell you, Olivia Berkeley, they are not trifles. They are second nature. Is it not cruel of God to make us so dependent on these wretched things? It was for these same wretched things that I endured torture for years—for money and clothes and carriages—just such things as that."

Olivia by a great effort recovered herself.

"What you say is true, Madame Koller. But I will not—how can you ask me such things about a man who has never—never"—she stopped at a loss to express her meaning, which implied a reproach at Madame Koller's want of delicacy.

Madame Koller made a gesture of impatience.

"What are promises?" she cried. "Nevertheless, I want you to see that if you marry Pembroke it will be his ruin. It would be most wicked selfishness."

"Madame Koller," answered Olivia, rising, "I will not listen to any more."

"I have nothing more to say," responded Madame Koller, rising too, and drawing her cloak around her. "I did not expect more from you than conventional tolerance. Had you a heart you would have felt for me—for him—for yourself. Can you conceive of anything more noble, or more piteous than two women, one of whom must make a great sacrifice for the man they both love—come, you need not deny it, or lose your temper—because I see you have a temper." Olivia's air and manner did certainly indicate dangerous possibilities. "I repeat, of two women as we are, the one makes the sacrifice—the other feels it to the quick. You talk though like a boarding-school miss. You might have got all the phrases you have used out of a book of deportment."

"I am as sincere as you are, Madame Koller," answered Olivia, in a voice of restrained anger. "I cannot help it that I am more reserved. I could no more say what you have said—" here a deep flush came into Olivia's face—"than I could commit murder."

Madame Koller stood up, and as she did so, she sighed deeply. Olivia, for the first time, felt sorry for her.

"Women who love are foolish, desperate, suicidal—anything. I do not think that you could ever love."

"Do you think that? I *know* better. I could love—but not like—not like—"

"Not like me?"

"Yes, since you have said it. Something—something—would hold me back from what you speak of so openly."

"I always said you were as nearly without feeling as the rest of the people here. Elizabeth Pembroke is the only woman I know of, among all of us, that ever really loved. But see how curious it was with her. She defied her father's curses—yet she did not have the nerve to marry the man she truly loved, because he happened to be an officer in the Union army, for fear the Peytons and the Coles, and the Lesters, and the rest of them, would have turned their backs on her at church. Bah!"

"I don't think it was want of nerve on Elizabeth Pembroke's part," replied Olivia. "She was not born to be happy."

"Nor was I," cried Madame Koller, despondently.

There was no more said for a minute or two. Then Madame Koller spoke again.

"Now you know what I feel. I don't ask anything for myself—I only wish to show you that you will ruin Pembroke if you marry him."

An angry light came into Olivia's eyes. She stood up, straight and stern, and absolutely grew taller as she looked fixedly at Madame Koller.

"This is intolerable," she said. "There is nothing—absolutely nothing—between Pembroke and me, and yet I am subjected to this cross-questioning."

"You would complain a great deal more of it if there were anything between you," answered Madame Koller, not without a glimpse of grotesque humor. "But now you know where I stand—and let me tell you, Olivia Berkeley, Pembroke is not guiltless toward me, however he would pretend it"—and without waiting for the angry reply on Olivia's lips, she vanished through the open door.

All that evening, as Olivia sat with a book on her lap, not reading, but watching the flame on the broad hearth, she was turning over in her mind what Madame Koller had said. It had disturbed her very much. It had not raised Pembroke at all in her esteem. She begun, nevertheless, to think with pity over the wretchedness of his fate should he be condemned to poverty. She fancied him harassed by debts, by Miles' helplessness. Her tender heart filled with pity.

"Olivia, my love," said the Colonel, emerging from behind his newspaper for a moment. "Pembroke means to try for the nomination to Congress—and Cave tells me he is pretty sure to get it. Great pity. A man who goes into public life without out a competence dooms himself to a dog's life for the remainder of his days. It ruined Pembroke's father thirty years ago."

Olivia started. This was like an oracle answering her own thoughts.

She thought, with a little bitter smile that it did not require much generosity to give up a man on whom one had no claim, and laughed at the idea of a struggle. At all events she would forget it all. It was not so easy to forget though. The thought stayed with her, and went to bed with her, and rose with her next morning.

Meanwhile, alas, for Madame Koller. When she came out, she looked around in vain for the negro woman who had come with her. She was not to be seen. They had come by the path that led through the fields, which made it only a mile from The Beeches to Isleham, but in going back, she missed her way—and then being a little afraid of the negroes, she went "around the road," as they called it. At the first gate, a man galloped out of the darkness. It was Pembroke. He recognized her at once, and got off his horse.

"You here," he cried in surprise—"at this hour"—for it was well on to seven o'clock, and Madame Koller was not noted for her fondness for walking.

"Yes," she answered.

"Is anything the matter at Isleham?" he asked—for she could not have come from anywhere else.

"Nothing at all," she replied nervously. "I—I—went over to see Olivia Berkeley," she added boldly.

Pembroke could say nothing. After a pause, Madame Koller burst out.

"Pembroke, that girl is made of iron. She cares nothing for you—for anybody but herself."

"And did you find out any of those things by asking her?" he inquired.

The twilight was so upon them that Madame Koller could not well see Pembroke's face, but she realized the tone of suppressed rage in his voice. She herself had a temper that was stormy, and it flamed out at that tone.

"Yes, I asked her. Are you a man that you can reproach me with it?"

It is difficult for a man, if he is a gentleman, to express his wrath toward a woman. Pembroke was infuriated at the idea that Madame Koller should go to Olivia Berkeley and ask prying questions. He ground his teeth with wrath as he looked at Madame Koller standing before him, in the half light.

"What a price I have had to pay for folly," he cried furiously. "A little damned love-making in a garden—" he was so savage that he was not choice of words and fell into profanity as men naturally do—"a half dozen notes and bouquets—Great God! Is there anything in that which should be a curse to a man's whole life! And I love Olivia Berkeley. I could make her love me, but—but for you."

His violence sobered Madame Koller at once.

"There was not much, certainly," she responded calmly. "The love-making in the garden and the bouquets would have been little enough—but unfortunately hearts are so perverse. A great many are broken by such trifles. It was very amusing to you but not so amusing altogether to me."

Pembroke began to be ashamed of himself. But he was still magnanimous enough not to tell her that she had taken a queer course about those things.

"I suppose I am to blame," he said with sulky rage after a moment. "I'm willing to shoulder all the blame there is—but why should Olivia Berkeley be insulted and annoyed by this kind of thing? Do you think you will ever accomplish anything by—" he stopped and blushed both for himself and her.

"One thing is certain," he continued. "After what you have said to Olivia Berkeley, questioning her about me, as you have admitted, I shall simply carry out my intention of asking her to marry me. She shall at least know the truth from me. But I think my chances are desperate. Pshaw! I have no chance at all. It's rather grotesque, don't you think, for a man to ask a woman to marry him when he knows that she will throw him over and despise him from the bottom of her heart?"

"That I must decline to discuss with you," quietly answered Madam Koller. She was indeed quiet, for at last—and in an instant, she realized that she must forever give up Pembroke. All that long journey was for nothing—all those months of wretched loneliness, of still more wretched hopes and fears, were in vain. She heard Pembroke saying:

"You had best let me see you home. It is too late for you to be out alone."

"You will not," she replied. "I will not permit you, after what you have said, to go one step with me."

Pembroke felt thoroughly ashamed. It was one of the incidents of his association with Madame Koller and Ahlberg that they always made him say and do things he was ashamed of. In short, they demoralized him. He had been betrayed by temper and by circumstances into things that were utterly against his self-respect—like this ebullition of rage against a woman. In the plenitude of his remorse he was humble to the last degree.

"May I," he asked—"may I, at least accompany you to your own grounds? It is really not safe for you."

Madame Koller turned upon him and stamped her foot.

"No, no—always no. Do you think there is any danger on earth from which I would accept your protection? Go to Olivia Berkeley. She would marry you in your poverty if it suited her whim, and be a millstone around your neck. Go to her, I say."

Pembroke watched her figure disappearing in the dusk along the faint white line of the road. He stood still with his horse's bridle in his hand, turning over bitter things in his mind. He thought he would not go to Isleham that night. He was depressed and conscience-stricken, and in no lover-like mood. He mounted his horse and rode slowly back to Malvern.

CHAPTER XII.

WHEN two weeks had passed, Pembroke still had not gone to Isleham—but in that time much had happened. The congressional convention had been held, and the ball had been opened for him by Cave with great brilliancy and power—and after a hard fight of two days, Pembroke had got the nomination for Congress. It was of infinite satisfaction to him in many ways. First because of the honor, which he honestly coveted—and again because of the ready money his election would bring. Modest as a congressional salary would be, it was at least in cash—and that was what he most needed then. He did not have a walk over. The parties were about evenly divided, and it was known that the canvass would be close and exciting. Pembroke warmed to his work when he knew this. It was like Bob Henry's trial—it took hold of his intellectual nature. He was called magnetic—and he had a nerve power, a certain originality about him that captivated his audiences.

There is nothing that a mixed crowd of whites and blacks at the South so much hates as a demagogue. Especially is this the case with the "poor whites" and the negroes. It was from them that Pembroke knew he must get the votes to elect. When he appeared on the hustings, he was the same easy, gentlemanly fellow as in a drawing-room. He slapped no man on the back, nor offered treats, nor was there any change in his manner. He was naturally affable, and he made it his object to win the good will of his hearers through their enlightenment, not their prejudices. The Bob Henry episode did him immense service. A great revolution had taken place in regard to Bob Henry. As, when he had been poor and in prison and friendless and suspected, everybody had been down on him, so now when he was free and cleared of suspicion, and had been an object of public attention, he became something of a hero. He worked like a beaver among his own people for "Marse French." At "night meetings" and such, he was powerful—and in the pulpits of the colored people, the fiat went forth that it "warn't wuff while fer cullud folks to pay de capilation tax fer to git young Mr. Hibbs, who warn' no quality nohow" into Congress—for the redoubtable Hibbs was Pembroke's opponent. This too, had its favorable action on his canvass. As for Petrarch, he claimed a direct commission from the Lord to send "Marse French ter Congriss. De Lord, de Great Physicianer, done spoken it ter me in de middle o' de night like he did ter little Samson, sayin' 'Petrarch whar is you?' He say 'What fur I gin you good thinkin' facticals, 'cep' fur ter do my will? An' it ain't Gord's will dat no red headed Hibbs be 'lected over ole Marse French Pembroke's son, dat allus treated me wid de greatest circumlocution." Petrarch's oratory was not without its effect.

Pembroke's natural gift of oratory had been revealed to him at the time of Bob Henry's acquittal. He cultivated it earnestly, avoiding hyperbole and exaggeration. There is nothing a Virginian loves so well as a good talker. Within ten days of the opening of the campaign, Pembroke knew that he was going to win. Hibbs had a very bad war record. Pembroke had a very good one. The canvass therefore to him, was pleasant, exciting, and with but little risk.

But Olivia Berkeley's place had not been usurped. He had not meant or desired to fall in love. As he had said truly to Cave, there were other things for him than marriage. But love had stolen a march upon him. When he found it out, he accepted the result with great good humor—and he had enough masculine self-love to have good hopes of winning her until—until Madame Koller had put her oar in. But even then, his case did not seem hopeless, after the first burst of rage and chagrin.

She would not surrender at once—that he felt sure, and he rather liked the prospect of a siege, thinking to conquer her proud spirit by a bold stroke at last. But Madame Koller had changed all this. He was determined to make Olivia Berkeley know how things stood between Madame Koller and himself—and the best way to do it was to tell her where his heart was really bestowed.

It was in the latter part of April before a day came that he could really call his own. He walked over from Malvern late in the afternoon, and found Olivia, as he thought he should, in the garden. The walks were trimmed up, and the flower-beds planted. Olivia, in a straw hat and wearing a great gardening apron full of pockets, gravely removed her gloves, her apron, and rolled them up before offering to shake hands with Pembroke.

"Allow me to congratulate our standard-bearer, and to apologize for my rustic occupations while receiving so distinguished a visitor."

Pembroke looked rather solemn. He was not in a trifling mood that afternoon, and he thought Olivia deficient in perception not to see at once that he had come on a lover's errand.

Is there anything more charming than an old-fashioned garden in the spring? The lilac bushes were hanging with purple blossoms, and great syringa trees were brave in their white glory. The guelder roses nodded on their tall stems, and a few late violets scented the air. It was a very quiet garden, and the shrubbery cut it off like a hermitage. Pembroke had selected his ground well.

Olivia soon saw that something was on his mind, but she did not suspect what it was. She had heard that Madame Koller was to leave the country, and she thought perhaps Pembroke needed consolation. Men often go to one woman to be consoled for the perfidy of another. Presently as they strolled along, she stooped down, and plucked some violets.

"I thought they were quite gone," she said. "Here are four," and as she held them out to Pembroke, he took her little hand, inclosing the violets in his own strong grasp.

There was the time, the place, the opportunity, and Olivia was more than half won. Yet, half an hour afterward, Pembroke came out of the garden, looking black as a thunder-cloud, and strode away down by the path through the fields—a rejected suitor. Olivia remained in the garden. The cool spring night came on apace. She could not have described her own emotions to have saved her life—or what exactly led up to that angry parting—for it will have been seen before this that Pembroke was subject to sudden gusts of temper. She had tried to put before him what she felt herself obliged in honor to say—that the Colonel's modest fortune was very much exaggerated—and she had blundered wretchedly in so doing. Pembroke had rashly assumed that she meant his poverty stood in the way. Then he had as wretchedly blundered about Madame Koller, and a few cutting words on both sides had made it impossible for either to say more. Olivia, pale and red by turns, looked inexpressibly haughty when Madame Koller's name was mentioned. Lovers' quarrels are proverbially of easy arrangement—but the case is different when the woman is high strung and the man high tempered. Olivia received Pembroke's confession with such cool questionings that his self-love was cruelly wounded. Pembroke took his dismissal so debonairly that Olivia was irresistibly impelled to make it stronger. The love scene, which really began very prettily, absolutely degenerated into a quarrel. Pembroke openly accused Olivia of being mercenary. Olivia retaliated by an exasperating remark, implying that perhaps Madame Koller's fortune was not without its charm for him—to which Pembroke, being entirely innocent, responded with a rude violence that made Olivia more furiously angry than she ever expected to be in her life. Pembroke seeing this in her pale face and blazing eyes, stalked down the garden path, wroth with her and wroth with the whole world.

He, walking fast back through the woods, was filled with rage and remorse—chiefly with rage. She was a cold-blooded creature—how she did weigh that money question—but—ah, she had a spirit of her own—such a spirit as a man might well feel proud to conquer—and the touch of her warm, soft hand!

Olivia felt that gap, that chasm in existence, when a shadowy array of vague hopes and fears suddenly falls to the ground. Pembroke had been certainly too confident and much too overbearing—but—it was over. When this thought struck her, she was walking slowly down the broad box-bordered walk to the gate. The young April moon was just appearing in the evening sky. She stopped suddenly and stood still. The force of her own words to him smote her. He would certainly never come back. She turned and flew swiftly back to the upper part of the garden, and stood in the very spot by the lilac hedge, and went over it all in her mind. Yes. It was then over for good—and he probably would not marry for a long, long time. She remembered having heard Cave and her father speak of Pembroke's half joking aversion to matrimony. It would be much better for him if he did not, as he had made up his mind to enter for a career. But strange to say this did not warm her heart, which felt as heavy as a stone.

Presently she went into the house, and was quite affectionate and gay with her father, playing the piano and reading to him.

"Fathers are the pleasantest relations in the world," she said, as she kissed him good-night, earlier in the evening than usual. "No fallings out—no misunderstandings—perfect constancy. Papa, I wouldn't give you up for any man in the world."

"Wouldn't you, my dear?" remarked that amiable old cynic incredulously.

CHAPTER XIII.

ONE of the drawbacks of Arcadia is that everybody knows everybody else's business—and the possibility of this added to Pembroke's extreme mortification. He thought with dread of the Colonel's elaborate pretense of knowing nothing whatever about the affair, Mrs. Peyton's sly rallying, Mr. Cole's sentimental condolence—it was all very exasperating. But solely to Olivia's tact and good sense both escaped this. Not one soul was the wiser. Olivia, however she felt, and however skillfully she might avoid meeting Pembroke alone, was apparently so easy, so natural and self-possessed, that it put Pembroke on his mettle. Together they managed to hoodwink the whole county about their private affairs—even Colonel Berkeley, who, if he suspected anything, was afraid to let on, and Miles, whose devotion to Olivia became stronger every day.

Luckily for Pembroke, he could plunge into the heat of his canvass. After he had lost Olivia, the conviction of her value came to him with overpowering force. There was no girl like her. She did not protest and talk about her emotions and analyze them as some women did—Madame Koller, for example—but Pembroke knew there was "more to her," as Cave said, "than a dozen Eliza Peytons." Perhaps Cave suspected something, but Pembroke knew he had nothing to fear from his friend's manly reticence. But to have lost Olivia Berkeley! Pembroke sometimes wondered at himself—at the way in which this loss grew upon him, instead of diminishing with time, as the case usually is with disappointments. Yet all this time he was riding from place to place, speaking, corresponding, as eager to win his election as if he were the happiest of accepted lovers—more so, in fact.

And then, there was that Ahlberg affair to trouble him. Like all the men of his race and generation, he firmly believed there were some cases in which blood must be shed—but a roadside quarrel, in which nothing but personal dislike figured, did not come under that head. Pembroke was fully alive to the folly and wickedness of fighting Ahlberg under the circumstances—but it was now impossible for him to recede. He could only hope and pray that something would turn up to prevent a meeting so indefinitely fixed. But if Ahlberg's going away were the only thing to count upon, that seemed far enough out of the question, for he stayed on and on at the village tavern, playing cards with young Hibbs and one or two frequenters of the place, riding over to play Madame Koller's accompaniments, fishing for invitations to dine at Isleham—in short, doing everything that a man of his nature and education could do to kill time. Pembroke could not but think that Ahlberg's persistence could only mean that he was really and truly waiting for his revenge. So there were a good many things to trouble the "white man's candidate," who was to make such a thorough and brilliant canvass, and whose readiness, cheerfulness and indomitable spirit was everywhere remarked upon.

One night, as Pembroke was riding home after a hard day's work in the upper part of the county, and was just entering the long straggling village street, his horse began to limp painfully. Pembroke dismounted, and found his trusty sorrel had cast a shoe,—a nail had entered his foot, and there was a job for the blacksmith. He led the horse to the blacksmith's shop, which was still open, although it was past seven o'clock, and on the promise of having the damage repaired in half an hour, walked over to the village tavern.

It was in September, and the air was chilly. The landlord ushered him into what was called the "card room"—the only place there was a fire. A cheery blaze leaped up the wide old-fashioned chimney, and by the light of kerosene lamps, Pembroke saw a card party at a round table in the corner. It was Ahlberg, young Hibbs, his political opponent, and two or three other idle young men of the county.

According to the provincial etiquette, Pembroke was invited to join the game, which he courteously declined on the ground that he was much fatigued and was only waiting for the blacksmith to put his horse's shoe on before starting for home. The game then proceeded.

Pembroke felt awkward and ill at ease. He knew he was in the way, as the loud laughter from Hibbs and his friends, and Ahlberg's subdued chuckle had ceased when he came in. They played seriously—it was écarté, a game that Ahlberg had just taught his postulants. Young Hibbs had a huge roll of bills on the table before him, which he somewhat ostentatiously displayed in the presence of his opponent, whose lack of bills was notorious. Also, Pembroke felt that his presence induced young Hibbs to bet more recklessly than ever, as a kind of bravado—and Ahlberg always won, when the stake was worth any thing.

The waiting seemed interminable to Pembroke seated in front of the fire. The conversation related solely to the game. Presently Pembroke started slightly. Ahlberg was giving them some general views on the subject of écarté. Pembroke himself was a good player, and he had never heard this scheme of playing advocated.

Over the mantel was an old-fashioned mirror, tilted forward. Although his back was to the players, Pembroke could see every motion reflected in the glass. He saw Hibbs lose three times running in fifteen minutes.

Pembroke's sight was keen. He fixed it on the glass and a curious look came into his dark face. Once he made a slight movement as if to rise, but sat still. A second time he half rose and sat down again—nobody in the room had seen the motion. Then, without the slightest warning, he suddenly took three strides over to the card table and, reaching over, seized Ahlberg by the collar, and lifted him bodily up from the table into a standing position.

"Produce that king of spades," he said.

If he had shot Ahlberg no greater surprise could have been created. Hibbs jumped up, dashing the cards and money in a heap on the floor, and nearly upsetting the table. One of his companions grabbed the lamp to save it.

Ahlberg turned a deathly color, and made some inarticulate effort to be heard, and tried to wrest himself from Pembroke's grasp. But it was in vain. Pembroke shook him slightly, but never relaxed his hold.

"The king of spades, I say."

Without a word Ahlberg reached down, and from some unknown depths produced the card. He was no coward, but he was overmastered physically and mentally. He knew in an instant that Pembroke had seen it all, and there was no shadow of escape for him.

Pembroke let go of Ahlberg's collar, and, taking out a white handkerchief, wiped his hands carefully. Ahlberg had sunk back, panting, in a chair. The grip of a hand like Pembroke's in the neighborhood of the wind-pipe is calculated to shorten the breath.

Hibbs looked dazed, from one to the other, and then to the floor, where the cards had fallen. The one damning card lay on the table.

"I saw it twice before this, in the glass," said Pembroke to Hibbs. "Each time I tried to catch him, but he did it so well I couldn't. But the last time it was perfectly plain,—you see. I could see under the table in the glass. You had better pick up your money, Hibbs."

At this, Ahlberg spoke up.

"All of it is Monsieur Hibbs'," he said with elaborate politeness, recovering his breath a little, "except two fifty-dollar notes, which are mine."

Pembroke picked out the two fifty-dollar notes and dashed them in Ahlberg's face, who very cleverly caught them and put them in his pocket.

"Mr. Pembroke," said Hibbs, stammering and blushing, "I—I—hope you won't say anything about this, sir. It would ruin me—I don't mean in the canvass, for I tell you truly, sir, I hope you'll be elected, and if it wasn't for the party, I'd give up the fight now. But my mother, sir, don't approve—don't approve of playing for money—and—"

"You are perfectly safe," answered Pembroke, "and quite right in your idea of duty to your party, and your dislike to wound your mother is creditable. But as for this dog, he must leave this county at once."

Ahlberg said not a word. He did not lack mere physical courage, but cheating at cards was, to him, the most heinous offense of which he could be convicted. He had been caught—it was the fortune of war—there was nothing to be said or done. At least, it happened in this out-of-the-way corner of the world, where it could never be known to anybody—for he did not count his acquaintances in the country as anybody, unless—perhaps—Madame Koller. At that he grew pale for the first time. He really wanted Madame Koller's money. But, in fact, he was somewhat dazed by Pembroke's way of settling the trouble. It really shocked his ethics to see one gentleman punish another as if he were a bargeman or a coal heaver. These extraordinary Anglo-Saxons! But one thing was plain with him—if he did not remain perfectly quiescent Pembroke was quite capable of throwing him bodily out of the window—and if he had lost his honor, as he called it, there was no reason why he shouldn't save his bones.

Pembroke, however, although he would have sworn that nothing Ahlberg could do in the way of rascality could surprise him, was as yet amazed, astounded, and almost puzzled by the promptness with which Ahlberg acquiesced in the status which Pembroke established. Ahlberg made no protest of innocence—he did not bluster, or grow desperate, or break down hysterically, as even a very bad man might under the circumstances. He simply saw that if he said anything, he might feel the weight of Pembroke's arm. Nothing that he could have said or done was as convincing of his thorough moral obtuseness as the way in which he accepted his own exposure.

Just then the landlord opened the door. "Mr. Pembroke, your horse is at the door. It's going to be a mighty bad night though—there's a cloud coming up. You'd better stay and join them gentlemen in their game."

"No, I thank you," replied Pembroke, and turning to Ahlberg. "Of course, after what has passed, it is out of the question that I should fight you. Good God! I'd just as soon think of fighting a jail bird! Don't take too long to get out of this county. Good night, Mr. Hibbs—good night—good night."

Hibbs accompanied him out, and stood by him while he mounted.

"Mr. Pembroke," he said, holding his hat in his hand, "I'm very much obliged for what you have done for me, and what you have promised. I promise you I'll never touch a card for money again as long as I live."

"And don't touch a card at all with such an infernal rascal as Ahlberg," answered Pembroke, altogether forgetting sundry agreeable games he had enjoyed with Ahlberg in Paris, and even in that very county—but it had been a good while ago, and Ahlberg had not tried any tricks on him.

This relieved Pembroke of a load of care—the folly of that quarrel was luckily escaped. But he debated seriously with himself whether he ought not to tell Madame Koller of Ahlberg's behavior, that she might be on her guard against him. In a day or two he heard, what did not surprise him, that Ahlberg was about to leave the country—but at the same time that Madame Koller and her mother were to leave The Beeches rather suddenly. Mrs. Peyton met him in the road, and stopped her carriage to tell him about Eliza Peyton's consummate folly in allowing that Ahlberg to stick to her like a burr—they actually intended crossing in the same steamer. That determined Pembroke. He rode over to The Beeches, and sitting face to face with Madame Koller in her drawing-room, told her the whole story. Pembroke was somewhat shocked to observe how little she seemed shocked at Ahlberg's conduct. It was certainly very bad, but—but—she had known him for so long. Pembroke was amazed and disgusted. As he was going, after a brief and very business-like visit, Madame Koller remarked, "And it is so strange about Louis. The very day after it happened, he was notified of his appointment as First Secretary in the Russian diplomatic service—or rather his re-appointment, for he was in it ten years—and he has come into an excellent property—quite a fortune in fact for a first secretary." Pembroke rode back home slowly and thoughtfully. He had never before realized how totally wanting Madame Koller was in integrity of mind. Olivia Berkeley now—

CHAPTER XIV.

IT takes a long time for a country neighborhood to recover from a sensation. Three or four years after Madame Koller, or Eliza Peyton had disappeared along with her mother and Ahlberg, people were still discussing her wonderful ways. Mr. Cole was paying his court mildly to Olivia Berkeley, but in his heart of hearts he had not forgotten his blonde enslaver. The Colonel was the same Colonel—his shirt-ruffle rushed out of his bosom as impetuously as of old. He continued to hate the Hibbses. Dashaway had been turned out to grass, but another screw continued to carry the Colonel's colors to defeat on the county race track. Olivia, too, had grown older, and a great deal prettier. A chisel called the emotions, is always at work upon the human countenance—a face naturally humane and expressive grows more so, year by year.

It is not to be expected that she was very happy in that time. Life in the country, varied by short visits to watering places in the summer and occasionally to cities in the winter, is dull at best for a girl grown up in the whirl of civilization. There came a time—after Pembroke, taking Miles with him had gone to Washington, when life began to look very black to Olivia Berkeley's eyes. She suffered for want of an object in life. She loved her father very much, but that cheerful, healthful and robustious old person hardly supplied the craving to love and tend which is innate in every woman's heart. It is at this point in their development that women of inferior nature begin to deteriorate. Not so with Olivia Berkeley. Life puzzled and displeased her. She found herself full of energy, with many gifts and accomplishments, condemned in the flower of her youth to the dull routine of a provincial life in the country. She could not understand it—neither could she sit down in hopeless resignation and accept it. She bestirred herself. Books there were in plenty at Isleham—the piano was an inestimable comforter. She weathered the storm of ennui in this manner, and came to possess a certain content—to control the outward signs of inward restlessness. Meanwhile she read and studied feverishly, foolishly imagining that knowing a great number of facts would make her happy. Of course it did not—but it made her less unhappy.

As for Pembroke, the fate which had fallen hard on Olivia Berkeley had fondly favored him. He was not only elected to Congress, but he became something of a man after he got there. The House of Representatives is a peculiar body—peculiarly unfavorable to age, and peculiarly favorable to youth. Pembroke, still smarting under his mortification, concluded to dismiss thoughts of any woman from his mind for the present, and devote himself to the work before him. With that view, he scanned closely his environment when he went to Washington. He saw that as a young member he was not expected to say anything. This left him more leisure to study his duties. He aspired to be a lawyer—always a lawyer. He found himself appointed to a committee—and his fellow members on it very soon found that the quiet young man from Virginia was liable to be well informed on the legal questions which the House and the committees are constantly wrangling over. Every man on that committee became convinced that the quiet young man would some day make his mark. This was enough to give him a good footing in the House. His colleagues saw that election after election, the young man was returned, apparently without effort on his part, for Pembroke was not a demagogue, and nothing on earth would have induced him to go into a rough and tumble election campaign. At last it got so that on the few occasions when he rose in his place, he had no trouble in catching the Speaker's eye. He was wise enough not to be betrayed by his gift of oratory into speech-making—a thing the House will not tolerate from a young member. He had naturally a beautiful and penetrating voice and much grace and dignity in speaking. These were enough without risking making himself ridiculous by a premature display as an orator. He sometimes thrilled when the great battles were being fought before his eyes—it was in the reconstruction time—and longed for the day which he felt would come when he might go down among the captains and the shouting, but he had the genius of waiting. Then he was a pleasant man at dinner—and his four years army service had given him a soldierly frankness and directness. He lived with Miles in a simple and quiet way in Washington. He did not go out much, as indeed he had no time. He became quite cynical to himself about women. The pretty girls from New York were quite captivated with the young man from Virginia. They wanted to know all about his lovely old place, especially one charming bud, Miss de Peyster.

"Come and see it," Pembroke would answer good-naturedly. "Half the house was burned up by our friends, the enemy—the other half is habitable."

"And haven't you miles and miles of fields and forests, like an English nobleman?" the gay creature asked.

"Oh yes. Miles and miles. The taxes eat up the crops, and the crops eat up the land."

"How nice," cried the daughter of the Knickerbockers. "How much more romantic it is to have a broken down old family mansion and thousands of acres of land, than to be a stockbroker or a real estate man—and then to have gone through the whole war—and to have been promoted on the field—"

Pembroke smiled rather dolefully. His ruined home, his mortgaged acres, Miles' life-long trouble, his four years of marching and starving and fighting, did not appear like romantic incidents in life, but as cruel blows of fate to him.

But Helena de Peyster was a pleasant girl, and her mother was gentle, amiable, and well-bred. They had one of the gayest and most charming houses in Washington, and entertained half the diplomatic corps at dinner during every week. They would gladly have had Pembroke oftener. He came in to quiet dinners with them, assumed a fatherly air with Helena, and liked them cordially. They were good to Miles too, who sometimes went to them timidly on rainy afternoons when he would not be likely to find anybody else.

So went the world with Pembroke for some years until one evening, going to his modest lodgings, he found a letter with Colonel Berkeley's big red seal on it awaiting him.

He and Miles dined—then Pembroke, over the wine, opened the Colonel's billet. It was brief.

"MY DEAR BOY,—Olivia and I are coming to Washington to spend the winter. I have not been to the cursed town since the winter before the war, when Wigfall was in the Senate, and Floyd was Secretary of War. John B. Floyd was one of the greatest men the State of Virginia ever produced. Now, I want to go to a decent tavern—but Olivia, who is a girl of spirit, won't do it. She insists on having a furnished house, and I've engaged one through an agent. Don't suppose it will suit, but Olivia swears it will. We'll be up in the course of a week or two, and will let you know. Damme if I expect to find a gentleman in public life—always excepting yourself, my dear boy. I inclose you our address. Olivia desires her regards to you and her particular love to Miles, also mine.

"Sincerely, your friend,

"TH. BERKELEY."

"That's pleasant news," said Miles.

"Very pleasant," replied Pembroke, without smiling in the least. He was glad to see the Colonel, but he was still sore about Olivia. Whenever he had been at home, the same friendly intercourse had gone on as before—but there was always an invisible restraint between them. Colonel Berkeley had noticed it, and at last ventured to question Olivia about it—when that young woman had turned on her father and cowed him by a look of her eye. There were some liberties the Colonel could not take with his daughter.

Promptly, the Colonel and Olivia arrived.

The house, which was after the conventional pattern of the Washington furnished house of those days, struck a chill to Colonel Berkeley's heart.

"My love," he said, disconsolately, looking at the dull grates in the two square drawing-rooms, "I'm afraid I'll lose all my domestic virtues around this miserable travesty of a hearth."

"Just wait, papa," answered Olivia, with one of her encouraging smiles.

"I knew how it would be. Wait until some of those big boxes are unpacked that you swore so about."

When the boxes were unpacked, they were found to contain the old fashioned brass andirons and fenders that had shone upon the cheerful hearths at Isleham for many years. Olivia in a trice, had the grates out and managed to have a wood fire sparkling where once they were. Then she produced a great porcelain lamp they had brought from France with them, and some tall silver candlesticks and candelabra, which vastly improved the mantels, and she re-arranged the tasteless furniture and bric-à-brac with such skill that she cheated herself as well as others into believing them pretty.

It was rather an effort to Pembroke, his first visit. He would not take Miles with him lest he should seem to fear to go alone. It was now five years past. Naturally they had met often, but in some way, this meeting impressed him differently. He had at last waked up to the fact that he could not forget Olivia Berkeley. It angered him against himself—and so it was in rather an unamiable mood that he left the House early, and took his way through a drizzling rain to the Berkeleys'. When he rung the bell, Petrarch's familiar black face greeted him.

"Hi, howdy, Marse French. It do my heart good ter see you. Ole Marse, I spec he everlastin' cuss when he fin' out you been here an' he ain't home. Miss Livy, she in de settin' room."

"And how are you all getting on here?" asked Pembroke, as Petrarch officiously helped him off with his great-coat.

"Tollerbul, tollerbul, sir. Old marse, he mighty orkard sometimes. He swar an' takes de Lord's name in vain, spite o' de commandment 'Doan never you swar at all.' I try ter make him behave hisse'f ter de policemens an' sech, but he quile all de time he gwine long de street."

He ushered Pembroke through the drawing-room, into a little room beyond. On a sofa drawn up to the wood fire, sat Olivia, making a pretty home-like picture, in the half light, contrasted with the dreary drawing-room beyond, and the dismal drizzle outside.

They had not met for nearly two years. The session of Congress had lasted almost through the year, and when he had been in the county last, Olivia was away in the mountains. He noticed instantly that she was very, very pretty, but her beauty had taken a graver and more womanly cast. Oh, the elaborate ease, to cover the overpowering awkwardness of those former tête-à-tête meetings! Pembroke felt this acutely when he first saw her—but it vanished strangely at the moment that Olivia held out her little hand and spoke to him. Her voice, her manner, were pleasantly natural. It carried him back to the old days when he was gradually slipping into love with her. How grateful and soothing had been her native charm as an escape from Madame Koller's exaggerated heroics!

"Papa will be sorry to miss you," she said pointing him to the easiest chair, and putting her feet comfortably on a footstool.

"Do you think you'll like it?" asked Pembroke.

"That's just what I was going to ask you."

"You mustn't ask me. You know Congressmen are received in society only on sufferance. I exist on the borders as it were, and am permitted to dwell there in spite of, not because I am a Congressman."

Olivia smiled and nodded her head.

"I know how it is," she said, "I've heard."

"Now what do you want to do first?"

"I think," said Olivia, propping her rounded chin on her hand, "I should like to go to a ball. I have not been to a real ball for six years—not since we left Paris. You may be surprised at this frivolity in one of my years—you know I am getting out of my twenties awfully fast—but it is still a fact."

"Your age is certainly imposing. There is a superb ball to be given at the Russian Legation next week—the Minister is a new man—just come. I received a card, and I can get one for you and your father through one of the secretaries of legation who is my friend."

Pembroke produced a handsome invitation card, bearing the name of the Russian Minister and Madame Volkonsky.

Olivia's eyes sparkled. She loved balls as the normal girl always does.

"And I shall go out to-morrow morning and buy a ball gown. Shall I have white tulle and water lilies, or peach-blow satin?"

"White, by all means," answered Pembroke, gravely. "I like to see women in white."

"A white gown," continued Olivia, reflectively, "is always safest."

"I suppose, you will go to balls all the time after this one. It will be like the first taste of blood to a tiger."

"Yes, after a long period of—what do you call it—graminivorous diet. By the way, some friends of yours came to see me to-day. The De Peysters."

"Yes, I like them very much. Helena is a charming little thing."

"Delightful girl," echoed Olivia, with much more emphasis than the subject required.

Pembroke had only intended to pay an ordinary afternoon call, but it was so unexpectedly pleasant sitting there with Olivia that the fall of night and the Colonel's return both took him unawares. The Colonel was delighted to see him.

"This is pleasant," cried he, standing with his broad back to the fire, and stroking his white mustache. "I brought my riding horse up, and Olivia's, too, and I sent Petrarch around this morning to make a permanent arrangement. The rogue of a livery man asked me such a stupendous price that I was forced to send him word I didn't desire board for myself and my daughter included with the horses. Ah, times are changed—times are changed! Sad lot of you in public life now, begad."

"Very sad lot, sir."

"If we could only get back to Old Hickory in the White House, and the mail twice a week from New York, brought in the stage coach—"

"And Old Hickory's *penchant* for Mrs. Eaton, and half the Congress getting tight at the White House New Year's Day. We ought to have it all."

"Yes—yes—Zounds, sir, we ought to have it all!"

Then there was the ball to talk about, and presently, Pembroke declining the Colonel's hearty invitation to stay and dine off whatever miserable fare a city market afforded, and try some port he had brought from Virginia, knowing there was nothing fit to drink to be had in Washington, he left. Olivia's invitation to stay was rather faint—had it been heartier, perhaps he might have remained. As it was, he went home, and surprised Miles by coming in whistling jovially.

CHAPTER XV.

THE night of the ball arrived. Olivia and her father, the De Peysters and Pembroke had all agreed to go in one party. The De Peysters had been very kind and attentive to Olivia. Her gentle ways had captivated Mrs. De Peyster, and the fun innate in her had done the same for Helena. They had asked Olivia to receive with them on their reception day, and she had made quite a little success on her first appearance in Washington society. She sat behind a cosy tea table in an alcove, and poured tea with much grace. She was a good linguist, and put two or three young diplomatists, struggling with the English tongue, at ease by talking to them in their own language. She possessed the indefinable charm of good breeding, never more effective than when contrasted with the flamboyant, cosmopolitan Washington society. The women soon found out that the men flocked around her. She had half a dozen invitations before the day was out. Helena, a soft, blonde, kittenish young thing, was in raptures over her, admiring her as only a very young girl can admire and adore one a little older than herself. Pembroke was among the later callers, and, strange to say, Miles was with him. There were but few persons there by that time, and these Mrs. De Peyster was entertaining in the large drawing-room. Helena brought Miles into the little alcove and plied him with soft speeches, tea and cakes. Pembroke and Olivia sitting by exchanged smiles at the two enjoying themselves boy and girl fashion. Helena was but nineteen, and Miles had not yet passed his twenty-third birthday. The horror of his wound was added to by the youth of his features.

"Now take this little cake," said Helena, earnestly. "I made these myself. Do you know that I can make cakes?"

"What an accomplished girl! I shall be afraid of you. I learned to make ash cakes during the war," answered Miles as gravely.

"What is an ash cake, pray?"

"Why, it's—it's—corn bread baked in the ashes."

"Oh, how funny! And how do you get the ashes off?"

"Wash them off."

In the course of the discussion Miles had quite forgotten a piteous and ineffective little stratagem of his to turn the uninjured side of his face toward whom he was addressing. He leaned forward, gazing into Helena's pretty but somewhat meaningless face, just as any other youngster might have done, and Helena, with youthful seriousness, had plunged into the sentimental discussion wherein the American girl is prone to fall. Pembroke would have gone after ten minutes, but Miles was so evidently enjoying himself, that the elder brother stayed on. It was like the afternoon at Olivia's house—so home-like and pleasant—Olivia and himself keeping up a desultory conversation while they sipped tea and listened half-amused to the two youngsters on the other side of the round table. Olivia glanced at the clock over the mantel—it was half-past six.

"I must go," she said. "I shall just have time for my dinner and for an hour's rest before I dress for the ball."

Mrs. De Peyster and Helena urged her to remain and dine, but Olivia declined, and the servant announced her carriage. Pembroke put her white burnous around her in the hall, and handed her to her carriage. They were all to meet at the Russian Legation at half-past ten.

At that hour the broad street in front of the Legation was packed with carriages. An awning for the waiting footmen extended on each side of the broad porte cochére. Half a dozen policemen kept the carriages in line and the coachmen in order—for this was the great ball of the season, a royal grand duke was to be present, and the fame of Madame Volkonsky's beauty had gone far and wide. The vast house blazed with lights, and amid the rolling of wheels, and the hubbub of many voices could be heard the strains of an orchestra floating out.

Almost at the same moment the carriages containing Olivia and her father, Pembroke and the De Peysters drove up, and the party vanished upstairs.

"How beautiful you are!" cried Helena delightedly, up in the dressing room, as Olivia dropped her wraps and appeared in her dainty white toilette, Olivia blushed with gratified vanity. Her dress was the perfection of simplicity, soft and diaphanous, and around her milk white arms and throat were her mother's pearls.

As the three ladies came out into the brilliant corridor to meet their escorts, Pembroke received a kind of thrill at Olivia's beauty—a beauty which had never struck him very forcibly before. She was undoubtedly pretty and graceful, and he had often admired her slight and willowy figure—but she had grown beautiful in her solitary country life—beautiful with patience, courage and womanliness. The Colonel, in a superb swallow-tail of the style of ten years past, his coat-tails lined with white satin, his snowy ruffle falling over the bosom of his waistcoat, his fine curling white hair combed carefully down upon his velvet collar in the old fashion, offered his arm like a prince to Mrs. De Peyster, herself a stately and imposing matron, and proud to be escorted by such a chevalier. Pembroke walked beside Olivia and Helena down the broad staircase.

Is there any form of social life more imposing than a really splendid ball? The tall and nodding ferns and palms, the penetrating odor of flowers, the clash of music, the brilliant crowd moving to and fro through the great drawing-rooms and halls, brought a deeper flush to Olivia's cheek. She felt like a débutante.

They made their way slowly toward the upper end of the last of a noble suite of rooms. Pembroke was just saying in low tone to the two girls, "I have looked out for your interests with the Grand Duke. My friend Ryleief has promised to present both of you—an honor I waived for myself, as being quite beneath the Grand Duke's notice, and—"

"Colonel and Miss Berkeley, Mrs. and Miss de Peyster; Mr. Pembroke—" was bawled out by Pembroke's friend, Ryleief who was making the introductions to the new Minister and his wife—and the party stood face to face with Ahlberg and Madame Koller.

The rencontre was so staggering and unexpected that Pembroke quite lost his self-possession. He gazed stupidly at the pair before him—M. and Madame Volkonsky, who had formed much of his life five years before as Ahlberg and Elise Koller. He saw Ahlberg's breast covered with orders, and he wore an elaborate court suit. Madame Koller, or Madame Volkonsky, blazed with diamonds. Her hair was as blonde and as abundant as ever, and far behind her streamed a gorgeous satin train of the same golden hue as her hair.

Olivia, too, felt that sudden shock at meeting people who rise, as it were, like the dead from their graves. She felt also that repulsion that came from a knowledge of both of them. She could only silently bow as they were presented. But both M. and Madame Volkonsky expressed more than mere surprise at the meeting. Ahlberg or Volkonsky as he now was, turned excessively pale. His uncertain glance fell on Pembroke, and turned again on his wife. As for her, the same pallor showed under the delicate rouge on her cheek, but women rally more quickly under these things than men do. Besides, she had contemplated the possibility of meeting some of these people, and was not altogether unprepared for it.

If, however, the blankness of amazement had seized upon Olivia and Pembroke, and if the De Peysters were also a little unnerved by the strangeness of what was occurring before them, Colonel Berkeley was as cool as a cucumber. He held out his hand warmly. He rolled out his salutations in a loud, rich voice.

"Why, how do you do Eliza. You'll excuse an old man, my dear, for calling you by your first name, won't you? And my friend Ahlberg that was. This is delightful," he added, looking around as if to challenge the whole party.

In the midst of the strange sensations which agitated him, Pembroke could scarcely forbear from laughing at the Colonel's greeting, and the effect it produced. Madame Volkonsky flushed violently, still under her rouge, while Volkonsky's face was a study in its helpless rage. Poor Ryleief, with a mob of fine people surging up to be introduced, was yet so consumed with curiosity, that he held them all at bay, and looked from one to the other.

"Does Madame understand that gentleman?" he asked in French, eagerly—

"Of course she does, my dear fellow," heartily responded Colonel Berkeley in English. "She spoke English long before she learned Rooshan, if she ever learned it. Hay, Eliza?"

The Colonel's manner was so very dignified, and although jovial, so far removed from familiarity, that Madame Volkonsky did not know whether to be pleased by the recognition or annoyed. If, as it was likely, it should come out that she was an American, here were people of the best standing who could vouch at least for her origin. She held out her hand to the Colonel, and said rapidly in French:

"I am very glad to meet you. I cannot say much here, but I hope to see you presently." When Pembroke made his bow and passed, Volkonsky called up all his ineffable assurance and gave him a scowl, which Pembroke received with a bow and a cool smile that was sarcasm itself. Madame Volkonsky did not look at him as she bowed, nor did he look at her.

In a moment they were clear of the press. The De Peysters were full of curiosity.

"Who were they? Who are they?" breathlessly asked Helena.

"My dear young lady," responded the Colonel, smoothing down his shirt-frill with his delicate old hand, "Who they were I can very easily tell you. Who they are, I am blessed if I know."

While the Colonel was giving a highly picturesque account of Eliza Peyton through all her transformations until she came to be Elise Koller, since when Colonel Berkeley had no knowledge of her whatever, Pembroke had given his arm to Olivia, and they moved off into a quiet corner, where the spreading leaves of a great palm made a little solitude in the midst of the crowd, and the lights and the crash of music and the beating of the dancers' feet in the distance. Pembroke was alternately pale and red. Madame Volkonsky was nothing to him now, but he hated Volkonsky with the reprehensible but eminently human hatred that one man sometimes feels for another. Volkonsky was a scoundrel and an imposter. It made him furious to think that he should have dared to return to America, albeit he should come as the accredited Minister of a great power. It showed a defiance of what he, Pembroke, knew and could relate of him, that was infuriating to his self-love. For Elise, he did not know exactly what he most felt—whether pity or contempt. And the very last time that he and Olivia Berkeley had discussed Madame Koller was on that April night in the old garden at Isleham—a recollection far from pleasant.

"Papa's remark that this meeting was delightful, struck me as rather ingeniously inappropriate," said Olivia, seeking the friendly cover of a joke. "It is frightfully embarrassing to meet people this way."

"Very," sententiously answered Pembroke. He was still in a whirl.

Then there was a pause. Suddenly Pembroke bent over toward her and said distinctly:

"Olivia, did you ever doubt what I told you that night in the garden about Madame Koller? that she was then, and had been for a long time, nothing to me? Did you ever have a renewal of your unjust suspicions?"

"No," answered Olivia, as clearly, after a short silence.

In another instant they were among the crowd of dancers in the ball room. Neither knew exactly how they happened to get there. Pembroke did not often dance, and was rather surprised when he found himself whirling around the ball room with Olivia, to the rhythm of a dreamy waltz. It was soon over. It came back to Olivia that she ought not so soon to part company with the De Peysters, and she stopped at once, thereby cutting short her own rapture as well as Pembroke's. Without a word, Pembroke led her back to where the Colonel and Mrs. De Peyster and Helena were. Helena's pretty face wore a cloud. She had not yet been asked to dance, and was more puzzled than pleased at the meeting which she had witnessed in all its strangeness. Pembroke good naturedly took her for a turn and brought her back with her card half filled and the smiles dimpling all over her face.

Meanwhile, the ball went on merrily. Ryleief escaped from his post as soon as possible and sought Pembroke.

"So you knew M. Volkonsky?" he said eagerly, in a whisper.

"Yes," said Pembroke—and his look and tone expressed volumes.

Ryleief held him by the arm, and whispered:

"This is confidential. I suspected from the first that our new chief was—eh—you know—not exactly—"

"Yes," answered Pembroke, "not exactly a gentleman. An arrant knave and coward, in short."

Ryleief, a mature diplomatic sprig, looked fixedly at Pembroke, his hard Muscovite face growing expressive.

"Speaking as friends, my dear Pembroke—and, you understand in my position the necessity of prudence—M. Volkonsky is not unknown among the Russian diplomats. He has been recalled once—warned repeatedly. Once, some years ago, it was supposed he had been dismissed from the diplomatic corps. But he reappeared about five years ago under another name—he was originally an Ahlberg. He certainly inherited some money, married some more, and took the name of Volkonsky—said it was a condition of his fortune. He has been *chargé d'affaires* at Munich—later at Lisbon—both promotions for him. What his power is at the Foreign Office I know not—certainly not his family, because he has none. It is said he is a Swiss."

"He will not be long here," remarked Pembroke. Then Pembroke went away and wandered about, feeling uncomfortable, as every man does, under the same roof as his enemy. He felt no compunction as to being the guest of Volkonsky. The legation was Russian property—the ball itself was not paid for out of Volkonsky's own pocket, but by his government. Pembroke felt, though, that when it came out, as it must, the part that he would take in exposing the Russian Minister, his presence at the ball might not be understood, and he would gladly have left the instant he found out who Volkonsky really was but for the Berkeleys and the De Peysters.

He stood off and watched the two girls as they danced—both with extreme grace. There was no lack of partners for them. Mrs. De Peyster, with the Colonel hovering near her, did not have her charges on her hands for much of the time. The truth is, Olivia, although the shock and surprise of meeting two people who were connected with a painful part of her life was unpleasant, yet was she still young and fresh enough to feel the intoxication of a ball. The music got into her feet, the lights and flowers dazzled her eyes. She was old enough to seize the present moment of enjoyment, and to postpone unpleasant things to the morrow, and young enough to feel a keen enjoyment in the present. She would never come to another ball at the Russian Legation, so there was that much more reason she should enjoy this one.

As Pembroke passed near her once she made a little mocking mouth at him.

"Your friend, Ryleief, promised that I should be introduced to the Grand Duke—and—"

"Look out," answered Pembroke, laughing, "he is coming this way. Now look your best."

At that very instant Ryleief was making his way toward them with the Grand Duke, a tall, military looking fellow, who surveyed the crowd with very unpretending good humor. Pembroke saw the presentation made, and Olivia drop a courtesy, which Helena De Peyster, at her elbow, imitated as the scion of royalty bowed to her. The Grand Duke squared off and began a conversation with Olivia. She had the sort of training to pay him the delicate flattery which princes love, but she had the American sense of humor which the continental foreigners find so captivating. Pembroke, still smiling to himself, imagined the platitudes his royal highness was bestowing upon the young American girl, when suddenly the Grand Duke's mouth opened wide, and he laughed outright at something Olivia had said. Thenceforth her fortune was made with the Grand Duke.

The next thing Pembroke saw was Olivia placing her hand in the Grand Duke's, and the pair went sailing around the room in the peculiar slow and ungraceful waltz danced by foreigners. Olivia had no difficulty in keeping step with her six-foot Grand Duke, and really danced the awkward dance as gracefully as it could be done. Mrs. De Peyster's face glowed as they passed. Olivia was chaperoned by her, and as such she enjoyed a reflected glory. The great maternal instinct welled up in her—she glanced at Helena—but Helena was so young—a mere chit—and Mrs. De Peyster was not of an envious nature. Colonel Berkeley felt a kind of pride at the success Olivia was making, but when a superb dowager sitting next Mrs. De Peyster asked, in a loud whisper, if he was "the father of Miss Berkeley," the Colonel's wrath rose. He made a courtly bow, and explained that Miss Berkeley was the daughter of Colonel Berkeley, of Virginia.

Not only once did the Grand Duke dance with Olivia, but twice—and he asked permission to call on her the next afternoon.

"With the greatest pleasure," answered Olivia gayly—"and—pray don't forget to come."

At which the Grand Duke grinned like any other man at a merry challenge from a girl.

At last the ball was over. Toward two o'clock Pembroke put the ladies of his party in their carriages and started to walk home. Madame Volkonsky had not been able to spoil the ball for Olivia.

"Good-bye," she cried to Pembroke, waving her hand. "To-morrow at four o'clock he comes—I shall begin making my toilette at twelve."

"Very pretty ball of Eliza Peyton's," said the Colonel, settling himself back in the carriage and buttoning up his great-coat. "Volkonsky—ha! ha! And that fellow, Ahlberg—by Gad! an infernal sneaking cur—I beg your pardon, my dear, for swearing, but of all the damned impostors I ever saw M. Volkonsky is the greatest, excepting always Eliza Peyton."

CHAPTER XVI.

WHILE Olivia might wince, and the Colonel chuckle over the Volkonsky incident, it was a more serious matter to Volkonsky. He had certainly taken into account the possibility of meeting some old acquaintances, but neither he nor Madame Volkonsky had cared to keep up with events in the remote county in Virginia, where they had passed some agitating days. Volkonsky therefore was quite unaware that Pembroke was in Congress. The first meeting to him was an unpleasant shock, as he had learned to fear Pembroke much in other days. But when he began to inquire quietly about him of Ryleief, who evidently knew him, Volkonsky's discomfort was very much increased. For Ryleief, who rather exaggerated the influence of a representative in Congress, impressed forcibly upon Volkonsky that Pembroke possessed power—and when Volkonsky began to take in that Pembroke's determined enmity as a member of the Foreign Affairs Committee might amount to something, he began to be much disturbed. Before the last guest had rolled away from the door on the night of the ball, Volkonsky and his wife were closeted together in the Minister's little study. Whatever passing fancy Madame Volkonsky might have entertained for Pembroke some years ago, Volkonsky was quite indifferent—and if Pembroke retained any lingering weakness for her—well enough—he might be induced to let Volkonsky dwell in peace.

When Madame Volkonsky entered the room, her husband placed a chair for her. Often they quarreled, and sometimes they were reported to fight, but he never omitted those little attentions. Madame Volkonsky's face was pale. She did not know how much lay in Pembroke's power to harm them, but she was shaken by the encounter. It was hard, just at the opening of a new life, to meet those people. It was so easy to be good now. They were free for a time from duns and creditors—for during her marriage to Ahlberg she had become acquainted with both. She had a fine establishment, a splendid position—and at the very outset arose the ghost of a dead and gone fancy, and the woman before whom she had in vain humiliated herself, and the man who knew enough to ruin her husband. It was trying and it made her look weary and very old. Volkonsky began in French:

"So you met your old acquaintances to-night."

"Yes."

"That charming M. le Colonel called you Eliza Peyton."

"Yes," again answered Madame Volkonsky.

"This comes of that crazy expedition to America which I tried to dissuade you from."

Madame Volkonsky again nodded. She was not usually so meek.

"And that haughty, overbearing Pembroke. Does he still cherish that romantic sentiment for you, I wonder."

Madame Volkonsky blushed faintly. She was not as devoid of delicacy as her husband.

"If he does," continued Volkonsky, meditatively, "he might be induced—if you should appeal to him—"

"Appeal to him for what?" inquired Madame Volkonsky, rising and turning paler. The contempt in her tone angered Volkonsky.

"Not to ruin us. That man is now in the Congress. He has to do with foreign affairs. He hates me, and, by God, I hate him. He knows things that may cause you to give up this establishment—that may send us back across the water under unpleasant circumstances. You know about the dispute at cards, and other things—you have not failed to remind me of them,—and if Pembroke is disposed he can use this with frightful effect now."

Madame Volkonsky remained perfectly silent. She was stunned by the information Volkonsky gave her—but Volkonsky was quite oblivious of her feelings. He was gnawing his yellow mustache.

"You might see him," he said. "You might appeal to him—throw yourself on his mercy—"

"What a wretch you are," suddenly burst out Madame Volkonsky in English. They had talked in French all this time, which she spoke apparently as well as English—but like most people, she fell into the vernacular when under the influence of strong emotion. Volkonsky glanced up at her.

"What is it now?" he asked, peevishly.

His wife turned two blazing eyes on him. The fact that she was not upon a very high plane herself did not prevent her from being indignant at his baseness—and wounded pride drove home the thrust.

"That you should dare, that any man should dare—to propose that a wife should work on a man's past liking for her to serve her husband's ends. Ahlberg, every day that I have lived with you has shown me new baseness in you."

This was not the first time Volkonsky had heard this—but it was none the less unpleasant. Also, he rather dreaded Madame Volkonsky's occasional outbursts of temper—and he had had enough for one night.

"It is no time for us to quarrel—and particularly do not call me Ahlberg. My name is now legally Volkonsky, and I would wish to forget it ever was anything else. We should better design how to keep this Pembroke at bay. I am sure," continued Volkonsky plaintively, "I have never sought to injure him. Why should he try to ruin me for a little scene at a card table that occurred five years ago? I wonder if that ferocious Cave will turn up soon?"

Madame Volkonsky turned and left him in disgust. In spite of her cosmopolitan education, and all her associations, there was born with her an admiration for Anglo-Saxon pluck which made her despise Volkonsky methods. The idea of scheming and designing to placate a man who had caught him cheating at cards filled her with infinite contempt.

In the course of the next few days, Madame Volkonsky was deeply exercised over the influence that Pembroke would have upon her future. She had talked their affairs over often with her husband in those few days. He had not failed to convey to her the rather exaggerated impression that he had received from Ryleief, as to Pembroke's power to harm.

One afternoon, when Volkonsky and his wife were driving in their victoria, they passed the Secretary of State's carriage drawn up to the sidewalk. Pembroke was about to step into it. The Secretary himself, a handsome, elderly man, was leaning forward to greet him, as Pembroke placed his foot on the step. Madame Volkonsky looked at her husband, who looked blankly back in return. The Secretary's carriage whirled around, and both gentlemen bowed—the Secretary to both the Minister and his wife, Pembroke pointedly to Madame Volkonsky.

Volkonsky turned a little pale as they drove off.

"I wonder if the Secretary will ever speak to us again," said Madame Volkonsky, half maliciously.

Yet it was as much to her as to him. It would indeed be hard were they driven in disgrace from Washington. Volkonsky had been surprisingly lucky all his life, but luck always takes a turn. Now, his recall as Minister would be of more consequence than his escapades as attaché or Secretary of Legation. Then, he had played wild works with her fortune, such as it was. Madame Volkonsky's thoughts grew bitter. First had come that struggle of her girlhood—then her artistic career—ending in a cruel failure. Afterward the dreadful years of life tied to Koller's bath chair—followed by her stormy and disappointed widowhood. This was the first place she had ever gained that promised security or happiness—and behold! all was likely to fall like a house of cards.

They paid one or two visits, and left cards at several places. Madame Volkonsky had imagined that nothing could dull the exquisite pleasure of being a personage, of being followed, flattered, admired. She found out differently. The fame of her beauty and accomplishments had preceded her. Everywhere she received the silent ovation which is the right of a beautiful and charming woman—but her heart was heavy. At one place she passed Olivia and her father coming out as they were going in. Olivia, wrapped in furs, looked uncommonly pretty and free from care. As the two women passed, each, while smiling affably, wore that hostile air which ladies are liable to assume under the circumstances. The Colonel was all bows and smiles to Madame Volkonsky as usual, and refrained from calling her Eliza.

Nor did the presence of the Volkonskys in Washington conduce to Olivia's enjoyment although it certainly did to her father's. The Colonel was delighted. In the course of years, Eliza Peyton had afforded him great amusement. He was a chivalrous man to women, although not above teasing Madame Volkonsky, but he refrained from doing what poor Elise very much dreaded he would—telling of her American origin. She had admitted that her mother was an American—an admission necessary to account for the native, idiomatic way in which she spoke the English language, and Colonel Berkeley knowing this, did not hesitate to say that in years gone by, he had known Madame Volkonsky's mother, and very cheerfully bore testimony to the fact that the mother had been of good family and gentle breeding. So instead of being a disadvantage to her, it was rather a help. But Olivia and herself were so distinctly antipathetic that it could scarcely fail to produce antagonism. And besides her whole course about Pembroke had shocked Olivia. Olivia was amazed—it was not the mere difference of conduct and opinion—it was the difference of temperament. Remembering that Madame Volkonsky had at least the inheritance of refinement, and was quite at home in the usages of gentle breeding, it seemed the more inexcusable. In all those years Olivia had been unable to define her feelings to Pembroke. She could easily have persuaded herself that she was quite indifferent to him except that she could not forget him. It annoyed her. It was like a small, secret pain, a trifling malady, of which the sufferer is ashamed to speak.

Not so Pembroke. The love that survives such a blow to pride and vanity as a refusal, is love indeed—and after the first tempest of mortification he had realized that his passion would not die, but needed to be killed—and after five years of partial absence, awkward estrangement, all those things which do most effectually kill everything which is not love, her presence was yet sweet and potent. The discovery afforded him a certain grim amusement. He was getting well on in his thirties. His hair was turning prematurely gray, and he felt that youth was behind him—a not altogether unpleasant feeling to an ambitious man. Nevertheless, they went on dining together at the Berkeleys' own house, at the De Peysters', at other places, meeting constantly at the same houses—for Pembroke went out more than he had ever done in Washington before, drawn subtly by the chance of meeting Olivia—although where once she was cool and friendly, she was now a little warmer in her manner, yet not wholly free from embarrassment. But neither was unhappy.

CHAPTER XVII.

A MONTH—six weeks—two months passed after the Russian Minister's ball. The Grand Duke had called informally on the President, accompanied of course by the Minister, but his visit to Washington was so brief that all formal courtesies were postponed until he returned from his travels in the Northwest, which would not be until spring. This was the time that Volkonsky looked forward to as deciding his fate. During the Grand Duke's first brief visit, Pembroke did not know of Volkonsky's diplomatic short-comings—nor until the last moment did he know that Volkonsky was Ahlberg. He was one of those intensely human men, who like fighting, especially if there is glory to be won—and he enjoyed a savage satisfaction in thinking that he would be the instrument of Ahlberg's punishment—and the prospect of the catastrophe occurring during the Grand Duke's visit, so there could be no misunderstanding or glozing over of the matter, filled him with what the moralists would call an unholy joy. He and Volkonsky had met often since the night of the ball, but never alone. The fact is, Volkonsky had his wife for a body guard. She was always with him in those days, sitting by his side in her carriage, or else close at his elbow. One day, however, as Volkonsky was coming out of the State Department, he met Pembroke face to face.

Pembroke had chafed with inward fury at the cleverness with which Volkonsky had managed to avoid him. Therefore when he passed the Russian Minister's carriage with Madame Volkonsky sitting in it alone at the foot of the steps, he was certain that Volkonsky was in the State Department, and that he could catch him—for it had assumed the form of a flight and a pursuit. Pembroke took off his hat and bowed profoundly to Madame Volkonsky. She could not but fancy there was a glimmer of sarcasm in his manner—a sarcasm she returned by a bow still lower. Pembroke could have leaped up the steps in his anxiety to reach the building before Volkonsky left—but he controlled himself and mounted leisurely. Once inside the door, he started at a long stride down the corridor, and in two minutes he had, figuratively speaking, collared Volkonsky.

"I want to speak with you," said Pembroke.

"With pleasure," responded Volkonsky, "but I may ask you to be brief, as Madame Volkonsky awaits me in her carriage."

"I will be brief. But I desire you to come to my club—here is my card—at six o'clock this evening."

Volkonsky straightened himself up. He determined not to yield without making a fight for it.

"Are you aware of your language, Meestar Pembroke?"

"Perfectly," answered Pembroke coolly. "Come or stay—do as you like. It is your only chance of getting away from the United States quietly—and this chance is given you not for yourself but for your wife."

Pembroke had kept his hat on his head purposely all this time. Volkonsky had removed his, but seeing Pembroke remain covered, put it back also. The two men gazed at each other for a moment, and then each went his way. But Pembroke knew in that moment that Volkonsky would come.

Once down in the carriage, Volkonsky directed the coachman to drive toward the country. It was a charming morning in early spring. Madame Volkonsky had expected to enjoy the drive, but when she saw Volkonsky's face she changed her anticipations.

"What did he say?" she asked, almost before the footman had mounted.

Volkonsky reflected for a moment, and then answered grimly:

"He has offered me a chance to get away quietly."

Madame Volkonsky said no more. Volkonsky began gnawing his mustache—a trick that Ahlberg had before. He did not speak until they were out in the country lanes. The fresh spring air brought no bloom to Madame Volkonsky's pallid face.

"But for the frightful insolence of the fellow," began Volkonsky after a while, "it might not be so bad. He is willing to negotiate. He has not gone yet to the Secretary of State with—with—his accusations. But the Secretary suspects me. I saw it in his face more plainly this morning than ever before. And there are certain things in connection with my negotiations—Great God! What a country! I communicate with the Department of State on certain diplomatic matters. The Department tells me that the Senate has called for information in the matter, and all my communications are handed over to a Senate Committee. Then the Lower House imagines there is a commercial question involved, and invites its Foreign Affairs Committee to take charge of it. There is no diplomacy in this miserable country," he cried, throwing out his hands. "The State Department is a puppet in the hands of Congress. No diplomatist can understand this when he comes here—or after."

"That is true," responded Madame Volkonsky, with a spice of sarcasm in her that never wholly left her. "None of you Foreign Office people know anything of the workings of the United States Government." This angered Volkonsky. He broke out—

"There is more yet to tell. This wretched *canaille* they call the Lower House, this Foreign Affairs Committee—is subdivided into numerous smaller committees—and the one in charge of our negotiation is virtually Pembroke—Pembroke himself!"

Madame Volkonsky fell back in the carriage. She did not wholly understand what this meant, but she knew from Volkonsky's manner, assisted by her own slight knowledge, that Pembroke was in some way the arbiter of Volkonsky's fate.

"And there are documents—letters—that Pembroke has called for, and the State Department has produced—that in the hands of an enemy—"

He struck his knee with his clinched fist. Disgrace stared him in the face—and the Grand Duke himself here—lying would do no good—and when that device would no longer avail him, Volkonsky felt that his situation was indeed desperate.

Both remained silent a long time. The carriage rolled along slowly. The road was smooth and bordered with beech and poplar trees, upon whose silvery branches the first tender shoots were coming out. The air was full of the subtle perfume of the coming leaves. But both the man and the woman were city bred. They neither understood nor cared for such things. Presently Madame Volkonsky touched her husband. Ahead of them they saw two figures. They were Olivia Berkeley and Miles Pembroke, walking gayly along the path, talking merrily. The sight of their innocent gayety smote Madame Volkonsky to the heart with envy. She had never been able to enjoy simple pleasures. A country walk, with a mere nobody, a boy younger than herself, with no one to admire, to notice, could never have pleased her. All her pleasures were of the costly kind—costly in money, in talents, in rank. She blamed fate at that moment for making her that way, and envied instead of despising Olivia.

The two by the roadside bowed—and the two in the carriage returned it smilingly. But the smile died the instant their heads were turned.

Volkonsky said presently to his wife:

"We must not show the white feather. You must sing to-night."

This brought Madame Volkonsky up with a turn. Her conversation with her husband had quite put out of her mind something that had engrossed her very much, and that was an amateur concert at the British Legation that evening, at which she was to sing, and for which she had been preparing earnestly for weeks. Singing, to her, was the keenest edge of enjoyment. She had begun to feel the delight of the applause, of the footlights, already in anticipation. It is true it was only an amateur concert—but it would be before an audience that was worthy of anybody's efforts—for was not everybody, even the President and his wife, to be present? And Madame Volkonsky had speedily found out that she would have no rival. She had looked forward with intense anticipation to this triumph—the one pleasure without alloy—the one chance of being justly admired and applauded. But in the last hour all had been forgotten. Even the artist's instinct was quenched. She turned cold at the idea of singing that night. But with her husband, she felt it was no time to quail. Then Volkonsky explained to her that he must meet Pembroke at six, and would afterward dine alone at home, while she would be on her way to the concert.

"And Elise," he said—he rarely called her by her name—"while there is yet hope—for he has not so far done anything, and I think he would not willingly make you miserable—if you have an opportunity, make—make an appeal to him."

Before, when the danger had not been so immediate, she had derided him to his face for this, but now, like him, she was ready to do anything. The sweets of her position had grown upon her. For the first time in her life she had commanded instead of asking admiration and attention. She made no promises, but Volkonsky knew that she was thoroughly frightened.

They went home, and Madame Volkonsky, directing that she be excused to visitors that day, went to her room. Like all people who have something to conceal, she hated and dreaded to be seen when an emergency was at hand. She lay all day on the sofa in her bedroom, ostensibly resting and preparing for the concert of that night—but she did not sing a note, and the professor of music, who came for a last rehearsal, was ruthlessly turned away like everybody else. In the midst of her own misery, Olivia Berkeley's calm and luminous face haunted her. Olivia's destiny was not a particularly brilliant one—the daughter of a Virginia country gentleman of modest fortune, condemned to a humdrum life for the best part of the year—already past her first youth—and Madame Volkonsky, wife of the Russian Minister, twice as beautiful as Olivia, gifted and admired—apparently everything was on Madame Volkonsky's side. And the two had begun life under much the same auspices. Madame Volkonsky, who was a clever woman in her way, was not silly enough to suppose that her present miseries had any real connection with the honors and pleasures she enjoyed. But being a shrewd observer, she saw that the excellent things of life are much more evenly divided than people commonly fancy—and she believed in a kind of inexorable fate that metes out dyspepsia and ingratitude and deceit to Dives, that the balance may be struck between him and Lazarus.

So all day she lay on the sofa, and thought about those early days of hers, and Olivia and Pembroke, and even her Aunt Sally Peyton and poor Miles and Cave, and everybody linked with that time. When she thought of Pembroke, it came upon her that he might be induced to spare her. She had never really understood Pembroke, although she had admired him intensely. If she had, things would have been very different with both of them. She never could understand her own failure with him. Of course she hated him, but love and hatred of the same person are not unfrequently found in women. She could not but hate him when she remembered that if he spared them and let them get away quietly, it would be because she was a woman, not because she was Elise Koller. But after all she would be rather pleased to get away from Washington now, if she could do so without being ruined. She wondered at her own rashness in returning. It seemed a kind of madness. There were pleasanter places—and it brought her early life and associations too much before her. She was not fond of reminiscences.

Occasionally as she lay upon the sofa, wrapped in a silk coverlet and gazing at the cheerful fire that blazed in the fireplace, she dropped into an uneasy sleep. This made her nerves recover their tone, and even somewhat raised her spirits. She was anxious and very much alarmed, but not in despair. About four o'clock her husband came into her room. His face was ashy and he held a dispatch in his hand.

"The Grand Duke arrives within half an hour. This dispatch has been delayed several hours. I go to the train now to meet him."

Madame Volkonsky sat upright on the sofa.

"Will it make—any difference to us?" she asked.

Volkonsky shrugged his shoulders.

"It will simply bring matters to a crisis. It may restrain Pembroke—if not, it is his opportunity to ruin me. I shall of course tell his royal highness and his suite of the concert, and they may choose to go. Russians must always be amused. Perhaps you will have the honor of singing for his royal highness as well as the President." His tone as he said this was not pleasant.

"I met the old Colonel Berkeley just now. He asked me how Eliza was. Is it that he is a fool or that he wishes to be impertinent?"

A ghost of a smile came to Madame Volkonsky's face. Her husband's total inability to understand Anglo-Saxon character, manners, sarcasm and humor could not but amuse her.

"Colonel Berkeley is not a fool at least," she replied.

Volkonsky went out and drove rapidly to the station. All the people attached to the Russian Legation were there, and in five minutes the train rolled in. The Grand Duke and his suite alighted, and the royal young man, taking Volkonsky's arm, entered his carriage and was driven to his hotel.

During all this time, Volkonsky was battling with his nervousness. He was afraid that the Grand Duke would invite him to dine—and in that case, he would miss Pembroke, and perhaps exasperate him. However the Grand Duke did not, much to the Minister's relief and the attachés' disgust. But the concert at the British Legation was mentioned, and the Grand Duke signified his august pleasure to attend. The Minister was to call for him at half-past eight—just the hour the concert began, but royalty does not mind little things like that. As the Grand Duke had not paid his respects to the President, the attendance at the concert was a little unofficial affair, that was to be made as informal as possible—under the rose as it were. At a quarter before six Volkonsky got off—and drove to the club.

Pembroke had not yet arrived, but the servants had orders to show M. Volkonsky to a private room, where Mr. Pembroke would join him. This delay enraged Volkonsky. He thought it was a premeditated slight on Pembroke's part to keep him waiting. He went to the room, however, and sat down and played with his gloves and waited impatiently and angrily.

It was nearly half an hour after Volkonsky had arrived that Pembroke came in looking hurried and flushed. He did not mind at all crushing Volkonsky, and could with pleasure have kicked him into the street, but he was not disposed to the small revenges, like keeping an enemy waiting. He said at once:

"Pray excuse my delay. I apologize—"

"No apology is required," answered Volkonsky haughtily; "I have this instant myself arrived. I have been in attendance upon his royal highness, the Grand Duke Alexis, who has just reached town."

"And I," responded Pembroke bowing, "have been in attendance upon his excellency, the President of the United States—which of course, obliges me to postpone any other appointment."

Volkonsky fancied a lurking smile in the corners of Pembroke's mouth. These incomprehensible Americans, he thought bitterly, never tell people when they are joking. But Pembroke was in no joking mood. He sat down by a little table between them, and looked Volkonsky full in the eye.

"I have been with the President and the Secretary of State, and it is upon your affairs that we met."

Volkonsky shifted uneasily in his chair. These terrible Americans. They outraged all diplomacy.

"And may I ask the result of that conference?" he inquired.

"Certainly. That if you will agree to go quietly, you may."

Volkonsky drew himself up. Pembroke remembered a similar gesture and attitude in a country road, some years before.

"And if I decline?"

Pembroke nodded gravely.

"Then the President, through the State Department will feel compelled to notify your government of the correspondence of yours which came into the hands of the Department, and was upon my request presented to the Foreign Affairs sub-committee. This is enough, you understand, for your recall, and perhaps dismissal. But I thought proper to inform the President of what *I* knew personally regarding you—and I also informed him that your wife was entitled to some consideration of which you were totally unworthy. So you had best take advantage of the President's leniency in allowing you to go, without a peremptory demand for your recall."

"You perhaps have gone too fast," answered Volkonsky in a quiet voice—for the whole conversation had been conducted in a conversational key. "You are no doubt aware that the United States Government is bound by some obligations to the Government of the Czar, owing to the stand taken by Russia during your civil war, when you, Mr. Pembroke, were in rebellion. If you will remember, when there seemed a strong probability that the Confederate government would be recognized by England and France, the Czar signified, that if such a contingency arose, he would be prepared to render the United States active help. As a guarantee, you will recollect the appearance of a small Russian fleet off the Pacific Coast. Now, upon the first occasion that a member of the royal family comes to the United States, to have a diplomatic scandal—to dismiss the Russian Minister the day after the Grand Duke's arrival—when arrangements are made for the presentations, and certain formal entertainments—will certainly be most awkward, and I may say, embarrassing, for his royal highness as well as the Russian Government."

"Quite true," answered Pembroke. "This phase of the question was discussed fully by the Secretary of State, who was present at the interview with the President. He mentioned that the strongest proof of friendship this Government could give the Russian Government would be for the Secretary to state privately to the Grand Duke how matters stand, and to offer, on his account, to permit your presence temporarily in Washington."

Volkonsky stood up for a moment and sat down again. His face was quite desperate by this time. And the amazing audacity of this American!

"How can it be arranged? It is impossible; you must yield," he gasped.

"The President himself has arranged everything. That is," he added, with some malice, "he agreed to my proposition, as did the Secretary of State. The Secretary, to-morrow, will have an interview with the Grand Duke, and—"

"Will follow the Grand Duke's wishes?" eagerly asked Volkonsky, rising again.

"Not at all," replied Pembroke, with dignity. "Such is not the practice of this government. The Secretary will notify the Grand Duke what the President is prepared to yield out of courtesy to the Russian Government, and respect for the Czar's family. You will be allowed to present the Grand Duke to the President, according to the original programme. But you will be careful not to offer your hand to the President, or to presume to engage him in conversation. Don't forget this."

"And the State dinner to his royal highness?" asked Volkonsky, in a tremulous voice.

"A card will be sent you, but you must absent yourself. It was agreed that you had abundant resources by which you could avoid coming, which I warn you will not be allowed. You might be called away from Washington upon imperative business."

"Or I might be ill. It would perhaps be the best solution of the difficulty if I should be taken ill now, and remain so for the next two weeks."

Pembroke could not for his life, refrain from smiling at this. Volkonsky, however, was far from smiling. He regarded these things as of tremendous import.

"And Madame Volkonsky—and the State dinner?" he said.

"That," answered Pembroke, with a bow, "rests solely with Madame Volkonsky. This government fights men, not women."

Volkonsky had been restless, getting up and walking about, and then sitting down at the table and resting his face on his hands. Pembroke had not moved from his first position, which was one of easy dignity. Presently Volkonsky burst out with:

"But did the President himself say anything of me?"

"He did."

"Then I insist on hearing it."

"M. Volkonsky, it would do you no good. The arrangements I have told you of are final, and I will be present with other members of the Foreign Affairs Committee at your meeting with the President."

Volkonsky at once thought that the President had said something which was favorable to him. He said violently:

"But I demand to know. I am still the accredited Minister of all the Russias. I have certain rights, which must be respected. I demand to know the President's exact language."

"M. Volkonsky, I expressly disclaim any sympathy with the President's remarks. His language is far from diplomatic. He did not expect it to be repeated."

"I demand to know," shouted Volkonsky, furiously.

"He said, he knew you were an infernal scoundrel the instant he put his eyes on you."

Volkonsky fell back in his chair almost stunned. Pembroke, whose sense of humor was struggling with his anger and disgust, almost felt sorry for him. After a pause, Volkonsky raised himself up and looked fixedly at Pembroke.

"Why do you not enter the diplomatic service?" he said. "You have great talents in that direction."

"Because," answered Pembroke, smiling in a way that made Volkonsky feel like strangling him, "the diplomatic service is no career for a man—"

"In America, yes. But in Europe?"

"Nor in Europe, either. Before the railroad and the telegraph, Ministers had powers and responsibilities. Now, they are merely agents and messengers. However, we will not discuss that. Our affairs are finished. I only have to warn you not to abuse the reasonable indulgence of this government. You are to take yourself off—and if not, you will be driven out."

After Volkonsky left him, Pembroke dined alone at the club. He felt singularly depressed. As long as he had Volkonsky before him, he enjoyed the pleasure of beating his enemy according to the savage instincts which yet dwell in the human breast. Volkonsky gone, he began to think with a certain remorse of Elise. The thought of her misery gave him pain.

Suddenly he remembered the concert. He recollected that Miles had engaged for both of them to go with Colonel Berkeley and Olivia. But for Miles, he would have excused himself from his engagement—but the boy could seldom be induced to go anywhere, and he had seemed eager to go to this place—but not without Olivia. For she had the gentle tact to make him feel at ease. She screened him from the curious and unthinking—he did not feel lost and abashed with Olivia as he did without her. So Pembroke finished his dinner hurriedly, and went back to his lodgings, where Miles was awaiting him, after having dined alone—and in a little while they were at the Colonel's house, where Olivia came out on her father's arm, and the big landau, brought from Isleham, with Petrarch on the box as of old, rolled along toward the British Legation and took its place in line.

When they reached the brilliantly lighted ball-room, where a concert stage had been erected and chairs arranged in rows, Pembroke took Miles' usual place at Olivia's side. He always felt with her, the charm of a sweet reasonableness and refinement. After the man he had talked with, and the thoughts and evil passions he had just experienced, it was refreshment to sit beside Olivia Berkeley, to look into her clear eyes and to listen to her soft voice.

The great ball-room was full and very brilliant. Pembroke looked and felt distrait. He was glad it was a concert, and that he could sit still and be silent, instead of moving about and being obliged to talk. He had altogether forgotten Madame Volkonsky's connection with it until he saw her name on the programme. It gave him an unpleasant shock—and presently there was a slight commotion, and the British Minister escorted the President and his wife up the room to the arm-chairs placed for them—and a few minutes after, the Grand Duke and his suite—and in the suite Pembroke saw Volkonsky.

Olivia did not look at Volkonsky as he passed. He always excited strong repulsion in her. Then the music began.

It was a very ordinary concert, as concerts are apt to be by very distinguished persons. The programme was long and amateurish. But when Madame Volkonsky's first number was reached the audience waked up. She was the only artist in the lot.

She came on the stage smiling and bowing, which raised the applause that greeted her to a storm. She need not have wished a better foil for her art as well as her manner and appearance than those who had preceded her. It had been her terror, amid all the pleasure of exhibiting her accomplishments, that the professional would be too obvious. She was always afraid that some practised eye—which indeed sometimes happened—would discover that her art was no amateur's art. But to-night she was troubled by nothing like this. She knew all. She knew that invited to the house of the President, she could not go—she knew that she must slip away like a criminal from her own country, and from those very men and women who now admired and envied her. She had married Ahlberg deliberately, knowing who he was, and had schemed with him and for him. She had done nothing very wrong, she had said to herself, a dozen times that day—nothing but to prefer present interest to ever-lasting principles—nothing but to join her fate with full knowledge, to a scoundrel—nothing but to have preferred money and pleasure and crooked ways to the straight. Meanwhile many women did as she did and were not so cruelly punished. But fate had overtaken her. No fear now lest people should know she was once a professional singer—they would know all about her soon enough. She knew that the storm that would break upon her was only delayed a little. She would therefore enjoy to the most this last time—this one feast at the king's table. She sang her best—sang as if inspired, and in the subtle harmonies, the deep mysterious cries, the passionate meaning of Schumann and Schubert, her soul found utterance through her voice. Had she been permitted to sing thus always—had that glorious but capricious voice always remained like that, she would have been a proud and satisfied artist, instead of this trembling and disappointed worldling, about to be hurled from her place in the eyes of the world she loved and feared so much.

The applause, which soon became as wild and earnest as if it were a real stage, warmed her and brought the red blood to her face. She bowed right and left with the grace and precision of one trained to receive applause beautifully. Then in response to the tremendous encores, she sang a little German song—so simple, so low and clear, that it sounded like a mother's lullaby. Even those arrayed against her felt the spell of her thrilling voice. Olivia Berkeley, who had always antagonized her strongly, felt her cheeks flush and her heart trembled with a kind of remorse.

Pembroke was pierced again, and more strongly, by the self-accusing spirit that this woman was to be stricken by his hand. He felt himself right in what he had done—but neither happy, nor self-approving, nor guiltless.

The rest of the concert seemed tamer than ever. When it was over there was to be a supper to a few invited guests. When the music came to an end, Pembroke rose, glad to get away from Madame Volkonsky's presence. But just then the British Minister came up and asked Colonel Berkeley and Olivia and the two Pembrokes to remain. Olivia accepted, but Pembroke was about to decline. He had begun in a deprecatory way, when Olivia said smiling, "You will be sorry if you go." Something in the tone, in the expression of her eye, conveyed more than the simple words, and fixed the fact in an instant that he would remain. He accepted, and almost before he knew it, he found himself near Madame Volkonsky, and the host invited him to give her his arm to the dining-room.

Like most women of her nature, Madame Volkonsky had a blind dependence upon what she called fate—which means upon any accidental conjunction of circumstances. She had been turning over in her mind, eagerly and feverishly, all day long the chances of five minutes' talk with Pembroke. She had not been able to hit upon anything that would insure it that night, because she had no warrant that she should see him—and even if he came to the concert, it was a chance whether he would remain to the supper. Again, everything pointed to one of the diplomatic corps taking her into supper—and only the charming indifference which the diplomatic corps manifests at Washington to diplomatic usages, could pair the wife of the Russian Minister with a young member of Congress. But in truth, the British Minister and all his diplomatic colleagues had got wind of what was coming, and it was an opportunity of giving Volkonsky a kick which pleased them all. The supper was quite informal, and the Grand Duke did not remain.

In the first flush of her joy at having a word with Pembroke, Madame Volkonsky entirely forgot the slight offered her by barring her out of a diplomatic escort. She was seated at a little round table where sat Ryleief, and by another strange turn of fate, Olivia Berkeley. Madame Volkonsky had drawn off her long black gloves and was talking to Pembroke with smiling self-possession, when she remembered that however Pembroke might rank as a man, she was entitled to go out to supper with a person of diplomatic rank. The British Minister might play tricks, as all of the diplomats did, with the Americans, but among themselves, etiquette was strictly observed, even at small and jolly supper parties. She was so well pleased with what destiny had done for her in giving her Pembroke as an escort, that she had no quarrel with destiny whatever. But with the British Minister and his wife, she did have a quarrel. She felt her anger and indignation rising every moment against them. It was the first stab of the many she was destined to receive.

Madame Volkonsky had most of the conversation to herself. Pembroke, in spite of every effort, felt heavy hearted. Olivia Berkeley was painfully embarrassed, and it required all her savoir faire to keep Ryleief from finding it out. As for Ryleief, he was so taken up with watching his three companions that he scarcely opened his mouth except to put something in it.

There was a great pretense of jollity at the little table—so much so, that Volkonsky turned from a remote corner into which he had been shoveled, with a faint hope that Madame Volkonsky had accomplished something. He was a hopeful scamp.

At last the opportunity came that Madame Volkonsky had longed for. They rose and went back to the drawing-rooms. She and Pembroke were in front, and by a gesture she stopped him in a recess under the broad staircase, that was half concealed by great palms. Perhaps Pembroke might have had a weak moment—but as Olivia passed him on Ryleief's arm, though she avoided his glance he saw her face—he saw a kind of gentle scorn in her delicate nostril—a shade of contempt that hardened his heart toward Madame Volkonsky on the instant.

In a moment or two everybody but themselves had gone. They were virtually alone.

"Pembroke," said Madame Volkonsky. The tone, and the piercing look which accompanied it, had all the virtue of sincerity.

"You know what I would say," she continued. "You have everything in your hands. You may drive me away from here—away from respectable society—away from all that makes life tolerable. What have I done to you that you should deny me mercy?"

"But I can do nothing now," responded Pembroke. "It is too late. And besides I have done very little. If I may say it, M. Volkonsky has done it all himself."

"Yes," answered Madame Volkonsky. "It is true he has done it all. But surely, you might make some plea. At least you might try. Oh, you cannot know what it is to feel one's self sinking, sinking, and not a hand held out to save."

Pembroke's face was quite impassive, but his soul was not so impassive. It cost him much to withstand the entreaties of a woman—and a woman who fancied she had some claim upon him, although in the bottom of his heart, he knew that he had got more trouble, pain and annoyance from Elise Koller than he had pleasure by a great deal—more bad than good—more war than peace.

"Madame Volkonsky," he continued, after a pause, "you are putting your appeal on the wrong ground. You will find that your husband has been mercifully dealt with—and that mercy was for your sake alone. Had you married him in ignorance—but Elise, you knew him as well five years ago as now."

Pembroke feared that his tone did not convey his unalterable decision, but it did, indeed, to the unfortunate woman before him.

"There is no pity in the world," she began—and then kept on, gasping with hysterical excitement. "No pity at all. I thought that you at least had a heart—but you are as cold—I never asked for mercy in my life that I was not denied. Even when I humiliated myself before Olivia Berkeley."

In the midst of her own frenzy of despair, she saw something in Pembroke's face that forced her to stop there. She was trembling violently and gasping for breath. Every moment he thought she would break into cries and screams. He took her firmly by the arm and led her to a side door, and out to where the street was blocked with carriages. Madame Volkonsky submitted without a word. It was useless. He was always so prompt. He had no hat, nor had Madame Volkonsky any wrap around her. He called for the Russian Minister's carriage, and in a moment it came. He placed Madame Volkonsky in it, and she obeyed him silently. Her head hung down, she wept a little, and was the picture of despair.

"Now, wait for the Minister," he said to the coachman—and he sent the footman for Madame Volkonsky's wrap.

Then he went back in the house, and through the drawing-rooms until he saw Volkonsky. "You had better go at once to your wife. She is waiting in her carriage," he said.

Volkonsky did not take time even to bid his host good-night, but slipped out, Pembroke a little behind him. When they reached the carriage, Madame Volkonsky was inside weeping violently. Pembroke had not got her out a moment too soon.

Volkonsky looked at Pembroke for a moment. "Madame has not her wrap," he said. "She has a mantle of sable that cost—ah, here is the footman with it." Pembroke turned away sick at heart.

Within a week the Grand Duke's visit was over, and the Russian Legation was suddenly turned over to Ryleief. The Minister was ill, and his doctors ordered him to the south of France. The day before Madame Volkonsky left Washington, a parcel was delivered into her hands. It was a rouleau containing a considerable sum of money. There was nothing to indicate where it came from.

"It must have cost a good deal of self-denial for Pembroke to send me this," she said, after counting the money. "He is not a rich man. It will perhaps serve me in some dreadful emergency"—for she had learned to expect dreadful emergencies by that time.

CHAPTER XVIII.

WASHINGTON society did not see much of Pembroke that winter. He worked very hard, and in the afternoons he took long, solitary rides. Sometimes in his rides he would meet Olivia Berkeley, generally with her father, and often Miles was with them. Then he would join the cavalcade, and exert himself to be gay—for it cannot be denied that he was not in very good spirits at that time. It is one thing to perform an act of rigid justice and another to take pleasure in it. Madame Volkonsky's last words rang in his ears.

He could not but smile at Olivia. She pierced his outward pretense of gayety, and saw that at heart he was sad. She fancied she knew why. By a mighty effort she brought herself to regard his infatuation for Madame Volkonsky with pity.

"It is written that Olivia shall always misunderstand me," he said to himself.

The Volkonsky matter did not end there. The treatment of the Russian representative suddenly presented a party phase. The party in power saw that capital could be made out of it. Pembroke had carried the whole thing through. Pembroke was a Southern man. Russia had offered her fleet during the civil war, in the event that France and England should depart from the strictest neutrality. It was easy enough to make the Russian Minister, who had departed, a martyr. In those unhappy days of sectional strife, these things were seized upon eagerly by both sides.

Pembroke heard that an attack was to be made upon him on the floor of the House. This gave him great satisfaction. He knew that his course was not only justifiable but patriotic in the highest degree. The question of Volkonsky's iniquities in the first instance had been thrust upon him by his political adversaries in the committee, who thought it at best but a diplomatic squabble. The sub-committee to which it was referred, had a chairman who was taken ill early in the session, and was not able to attend any of the committee meetings. His other colleague was incurably lazy—so this supposed trifling matter was wholly in his hands, and it had turned out a first-class sensation.

The visit of the Grand Duke, and the complications from Russia's extreme friendliness toward the Government at a critical time, had suddenly made the question assume a phase of international importance. Without scandal, and without giving offense, the State Department, acting on Pembroke's information, had managed to rout Volkonsky, and incidentally to give a warning to continental governments regarding the men they should send as diplomatic representatives to the United States. The Secretary of State, a cold, formal, timid, but dignified man, was infinitely gratified and relieved at the manner in which Pembroke had managed Volkonsky.

The President had laughed with grim humor at the account of Volkonsky's utter rout. Altogether it was a chain of successes for Pembroke, and it gave him his opportunity to show the debater's stuff there was in him. Therefore, when he was informed that on a certain day he would have to answer for himself on the floor of the House, he felt in high spirits, for the first time in weeks.

Miles was full of excitement. Colonel Berkeley, whose sectionalism was of the robust and aggressive kind indigenous in Virginia, was in high feather. He charged Pembroke repeatedly to wallop those infernal Yankees so that they would never forget it, and recalled all the forensic glories of all the Pembrokes to him. Olivia brightened into wonderful interest. She said it was the subject that interested her.

The evening before the resolution was to be called up, Pembroke walked over to the Berkeleys, Olivia and her father sat in the cosy library. The Colonel began immediately.

"My dear fellow, you ought not to be here this minute. Remember you have got to speak for the State of Virginia to-morrow. You ought to be sharpening your blade and seeing to the joints in your armor."

"You should, indeed," struck in Olivia, with great animation. "You can't imagine how nervous I feel. You see, you are to be the mouth-piece of all of us. If you don't do your best, and show that we have some patriotism, as well as the North, I believe there will be a general collapse among all the Southern people here."

Pembroke could not help laughing.

"Your anxiety, Colonel, and Miss Berkeley's doesn't bespeak great confidence in me."

Olivia blushed and protested more earnestly.

"Not so, not so, sir," cried the Colonel. "We have every confidence in you, but my boy, you had better take a look at Cicero's orations against Catiline—and read over to-night Sheridan's speeches—and Hayne against Webster."

Pembroke threw himself back in his chair, and his laugh was so boyish and hearty, that Olivia was startled into joining in it.

"This is fearful," said Olivia, bringing her pretty brows together sternly. "This is unpardonable levity. At a time like this, it is dreadful for us to stand so in awe of your self-love. Really now, we know that you are eloquence and cleverness itself, but it isn't safe," she continued, with an air of infinite experience, "to trust anything to chance."

"Come down to the House to-morrow and encourage me," replied Pembroke good humoredly, "and keep up Miles' spirits when I begin to flounder."

The evening was very jolly, like those old ones in Paris and in Virginia. Pembroke at last rose to go, and in parting, the Colonel clapped him on the back, while Olivia held his hand and pressed it so warmly that Pembroke's dark face colored with pleasure, as she said:

"Now, I know I am offending you—but you can't imagine how frightened I am. You may come out all right—but the suspense will be dreadful—" She was laughing, too, but Pembroke saw under her badinage a powerful interest in his success. He went away elated. "At least she will see that I was worthy of more consideration than she gave me," he thought—a common reflection to men who have been refused.

Next day the floor of the House was crowded and the galleries packed. Administration and anti-administration people were interested. Society turned out in force to hear the revelations about the late Russian Minister—the private and diplomatic galleries were filled. The Senate was not in session, and many Senators were on the floor.

After the morning hour, and the droning through of some unimportant business, the leader of the majority rose, and demanded the consideration of the resolution of inquiry relating to the recall of the Russian Minister from this country. At that a hush fell upon the crowd. The leader of the opposition rose to reply. He stated briefly that it was a matter concerning the Foreign Affairs Committee, and a member of one of the sub-committees had sole charge of it owing to the illness of the chairman. Another member then rose, and sarcastically referring to the fact that the gentleman referred to could scarcely be supposed to entertain friendly feelings toward the representative of the only foreign government which showed the slightest sympathy toward the Union in the Civil War, demanded to know by what right had the Russian Minister's position in Washington been made untenable—and that too, at the time of the visit of a member of the Czar's family—and was this the return the United States Government made for the Czar's extreme friendliness? Then Pembroke stood up in his place, at a considerable distance from the Speaker. This gave him a great advantage, for it showed the fine resonant quality of his voice, clear and quite free from rant and harshness. Olivia Berkeley, who watched him from the front row in the gallery, saw that he was pale, but perfectly self-possessed. As he caught her eye, in rising, he smiled at her.

"Mr. Speaker."

The Speaker fixed his piercing eyes upon him, and with a light tap of the gavel, said "The gentleman from Virginia has the floor."

Pembroke used no notes. He began in a clear and dignified manner to recite the part taken by him in Volkonsky's case—his suspicions, his demand for documents from the State Department, Volkonsky's compromising letters, of which he read copies—the dilemma of the Department, anxious not to offend Russia but indignant at the baseness of Volkonsky—the further complication of the Grand Duke's visit, and all which followed. He then read his statement of what had occurred at his interviews with Volkonsky, and which he had filed at the State Department.

"And here let me say," he remarked, pausing from the reading of his minutes of his last conversation with Volkonsky, "that in some of my language and stipulations I had no authority from either the President or Secretary of State—but with the impetuosity of all honest men, I felt a profound indignation at a man of the late Minister's character, daring to present himself as an accredited agent to this Government. In many of these instances, as for example, when I stipulated that the late Minister should not presume to shake hands with the President at his parting interview, or address him in any way, no doubt the late Minister supposed that I was instructed to make that stipulation. Sir, I was not. It was an outburst of feeling. I felt so clearly that no man of Volkonsky's character should be permitted to touch the hand of the President of the United States, that I said so—and said so in such a way that the late Minister supposed I had the President's authority for it."

At this, there was an outburst of applause. The Speaker made no move to check it. Pembroke bowed slightly, and resumed in his calm and piercing voice.

Members of the House and Senate had settled themselves to hear a speech. In five minutes the old stagers had found out that there was the making of a great parliamentary speaker in this stalwart dark young man. Members leaned back and touched each other. Pens refrained from scratching. The pages, finding nothing to do, crept toward the Speaker's desk and sat down on the carpeted steps. One little black-eyed fellow fixed his gaze on Pembroke's face, and at the next point he made, the page, without waiting for his elders, suddenly clapped furiously. A roar of laughter and applause followed. Pembroke smiled, and did not break silence again until the Speaker gave him a slight inclination of the head. In that pause he had glanced at Olivia in the gallery. Her face was crimson with pride and pleasure.

Outside in the corridors, the word had gone round that there was something worth listening to going on inside. The aisles became packed. A slight disturbance behind him showed Pembroke that a contingent of women was being admitted to the floor—and before him, in the reporters' gallery, where men were usually moving to and fro, every man was at his post, and there was no passing in and out.

Pembroke began to feel a sense of triumph. His easy, but forcible delivery was not far from eloquence. He felt the pulse of his audience, as it were. At first, when he began, it was entirely cold and critical, while his blood leaped like fire through his veins, and it took all his will-power to maintain his appearance of coolness. But as his listeners warmed up, he cooled off. The more subtly he wrought them up, the more was he master of himself. His nerve did not once desert him.

Gradually he began to lead up to where he hoped to make his point—that, although of the party in opposition, he felt as deeply, and resented as instantly, any infringement of the dignity of the Government as any citizen of the republic—and that such was the feeling in his party. His own people saw his lead and applauded tremendously. Just then the Speaker's gavel fell. Loud cries of "Go on! Go on! Give him half an hour more! Give him an hour!" rang out. Pembroke had ceased in the middle of a sentence, and had sat down.

"Is there objection to the gentleman from Virginia continuing?" asked the Speaker, in an animated voice. "The Chair hears none. The gentleman will proceed."

The applause now turned into cheers and shouts. One very deaf old gentleman moved forward to Pembroke and, deliberately motioning a younger man out of his seat, quietly took possession of it, to the amusement of the House. The little page, who was evidently a pet of the old gentleman, stole up to him and managed to crowd in the same chair. Shouts of laughter followed this, followed by renewed applause for Pembroke, in which his opponents good-naturedly joined. Then Pembroke felt that the time had come. He had the House with him.

He spoke for an hour. He merely took the Volkonsky incident for a text. He spoke of the regard for the common weal exhibited by his party, and he vigorously denounced his opponents for their attempt to make party capital out of that which was near and dear to all Americans. He spoke with temper and judgment, but his party realized that they had gained a powerful aid in their fight with the majority. At the last he artfully indulged in one burst of eloquence—in which he seemed carried away by his theme, but in which, like a genuine orator, he played upon his audience, and while they imagined that he had forgotten himself he was watching them. Truly they had forgotten everything but the ringing words of the speaker. He had touched the chord of true Americanism which sweeps away all parties, all prejudices. Then, amidst prolonged and vociferous cheering, he sat down. Senators and Representatives closed around him, congratulating him and shaking hands. The House was in no mood for anything after that, and a motion to adjourn was carried, nobody knew how. When at last, to escape being made to appear as if he remained to be congratulated, Pembroke was going toward the cloak room the Speaker passed near him and advanced and offered his hand. "Ah," he cried, in his pleasant, jovial way, "right well have you acquitted yourself this day. You'll find much better company on our side of the House, however, my young friend."

"Thank you," said Pembroke, smiling and bowing to the great man. "It's not bad on my own side."

The Speaker laughed and passed on.

Pembroke slipped out. It was a pleasant spring afternoon. The world took on for him a glorious hue just then, as it does to every man who finds his place in life, and that place an honorable one. But one thing was wanting—a tender heart to sympathize with him at that moment. Instead of turning toward his lodgings, he walked away into the country—away where he could see the blue line of the Virginia hills. It gave him a kind of malicious satisfaction, and was yet pain to him, that Olivia would be expecting him, and that she should be disappointed. As the hero of the hour she would naturally want to greet him.

"Well," he thought, as he struck out more vigorously still, "let us see if my lady will not peak and pine a little at being forgotten." And yet her hurt gave him hurt, too. Love and perversity are natural allies.

It was quite dark when he returned to his lodgings. Miles was not there—gone to dinner with the Berkeleys.

About ten o'clock Miles turned up, the proudest younger brother in all America. He had all that he had heard to tell his brother. But presently he asked:

"Why didn't you come to the Berkeleys'? The Colonel kept the carriage waiting at the Capitol for you. Olivia listened at dinner for your step, and jumped up once, thinking you had come."

"I needed a walk in the country," answered Pembroke, sententiously.

Miles sighed. A look came into his poor face that Pembroke had seen there before—a look that made the elder brother's strong heart ache. Any disappointment to Olivia was a stab to this unfortunate young soul. Men, as nature made them, are not magnanimous in love. Only some frightful misfortune like this poor boy's can make them so.

Presently Miles continued, hesitatingly:

"You must go to see her very early to-morrow. You know they return to Virginia early in the week."

"I can't go," answered Pembroke, wounding himself, and the brother that he loved better than himself, in order to wound Olivia. "I must go to New York early to-morrow morning, on business. I was notified ten days ago."

Miles said no more.

Early the next morning Pembroke was off, leaving a note for Olivia, which that young lady showed her father, and then, running up to her own room, tore into bits—and then she burst into tears. And yet it was a most kind, cordial, friendly note. When Pembroke returned, the Berkeleys had left town for the season.

CHAPTER XIX.

THE quaint old house, and the straggling, half-kept grounds at Isleham were never lovelier than that spring. Sometimes the extreme quiet and repose had weighed upon Olivia's spirits as it would upon any other young and vigorous nature. But now she had a good deal of a certain sort of excitement. She was country-bred, and naturally turned to the country for any home feeling she might have. The Colonel and Petrarch were a little bored at first. Both missed the social life at Washington. Pete had been a success in his own circle. His ruffled shirt-front, copied from his master's, had won infinite respect among his own color. As for the natty white footmen and coachmen, their opinion and treatment, even their jeers, he regarded with lofty indifference, and classed them as among the poorest of poor white trash.

His religion, too, had struck terror to those of the Washington darkies to whom he had had a chance to expound it. His liberal promises of eternal damnation, "an' sizzlin' an' fryin' in perdition, wid de devil bastin' 'em wid de own gravy," had not lost force even through much repetition. "Ole marse," Petrarch informed Olivia, "he cuss 'bout dem dam towns, an' say he aint had nuttin' fittin' ter eat sence he lef' Verginny. Ole marse, he jis' maraudin' an' cussin' 'cause he aint got nuttin' ter do. I lay he gwi' back naix' year. Ef he does, I got some preachments ter make ter dem wuffless niggers d'yar, totin' de sins 'roun' like twuz' gol' an' silver."

It seemed as if Olivia were destined to suffer a good deal of secret mortification on Pembroke's account. That last neglect of his had cut her to the soul. She had waked up to the fact, however, that Pembroke had taken his first rebuff in good earnest, and that nothing was left for her but that hollow pretense of friendship which men and women who have been, or have desired to be, more to each other, must affect. It was rather a painful and uncomfortable feeling to take around with her, when listening to Mrs. Peyton's vigorous talk, or the Rev. Mr. Cole's harmless sermons, and still more harmless conversation. But it was there, and it was unconquerable, and she must simply adjust the burden that she might bear it.

The county was full of talk about Pembroke's speech. The older people were sure that some information of his father's great speeches in their court-house about 1849 must have reached Washington, and that Pembroke's future was predicated upon them. Then there was a good deal in the newspapers about it. The Richmond papers printed the speech in full, together with a genealogical sketch of his family since the first Pembroke came over, with a grant of land from Charles the Second in his pocket. Likewise, Pembroke's success was attributed almost wholly to his ancestry, and he himself was considered to have had a merely nominal share in it.

It was the long session of Congress, and there was no talk of Pembroke's returning to the county. Whenever he did come, though, it was determined to give him a public dinner.

One afternoon in May, about the same time of year that Pembroke and Olivia had had their pointed conversation in the garden, Olivia was trimming her rose-bushes. She was a famous gardener, and a part of every morning and afternoon she might have been found looking after her shrubs and flowers. Sometimes, with a small garden hoe, she might have been seen hoeing vigorously, much to Petrarch's disgust, who remonstrated vainly.

"Miss 'Livy, yo' mar never did no sech a thing. When she want hoein' done, she sen' fur Susan's Torm, an' Simon Peter an' Unc' Silas' Jake. She didn't never demean herself wid no hoe in her han'."

"But I haven't got Susan's Tom, nor Simon Peter nor Uncle Silas' Jake. And besides, I am doing it because I like it."

"Fur Gord A'mighty's sake, Miss 'Livy, doan' lemme hear dat none o' de Berkeleys likes fur ter wuk. De Berkeleys allus wuz de gentlefolks o' de county. Didn't none on 'em like ter wuk. Ketch ole marse wukkin! Gord warn't conjurin' 'bout de fust families when He say, 'By de sweat o' de brow dey shall scuffle fer de vittals.' He mos' p'intedly warn't studyin' 'bout de Berkeleys, 'kase dey got dat high an' mighty sperrit dey lay down an' starve 'fo' dey disqualify deyselfs by wukkin'."

But Olivia stuck bravely to her plebeian amusement. On this particular afternoon she was not hoeing. She was merely snipping off straggling wisps from the great rose-trees—old-fashioned "maiden's blush," and damasks. She was thinking, as, indeed, she generally did when she found herself employed in that way, of Pembroke and that unlucky afternoon six years ago.

Before she knew it Pembroke was advancing up the garden walk. In a moment they were shaking hands with a great assumption of friendliness. Olivia could not but wonder if he remembered the similarity between that and just such another spring afternoon in the same place. Pembroke looked remarkably well and seemed in high spirits.

"The Colonel was out riding—and I did not need Pete's directions to know that you were very likely pottering among your flowers at this time."

"Pottering is such a senile kind of a word—you make me feel I am in my dotage. Doddering is the next step to pottering. And this, I remember, is the first chance I have had to congratulate you in person on your speech. Papa gives your father and your grandfather the whole credit. I asked him, however, when he wrote you to give my congratulations."

"Which he did. It was a very cold and clammy way of felicitating a friend."

Olivia said nothing, but she could not restrain an almost imperceptible lifting of the brows.

"The result of that speech has been," continued Pembroke, after a little pause, "that I am in public life to stay as long as I can. That means that I shall never be a rich man. Honest men, in these times, don't get rich on politics."

A brilliant blush came into Olivia's face at that. In the midst of suggestive circumstances Pembroke seemed determined to add suggestive remarks.

"But I hardly think you could take that into consideration," she answered, after a moment. "A man's destiny is generally fixed by his talents. You will probably not make a great fortune, but you may make a great reputation—and to my way of thinking the great reputation is the more to be coveted."

"Did you always think so?"

"Always."

Then there came an awkward pause. Olivia was angry with him for asking the first question, but Pembroke seemed determined to pursue it.

"Even when I asked you to marry me on this very spot, six years ago? Then I understood that you could not marry a poor man."

"Then," said Olivia, calmly, and facing him, "you very much misunderstood me. I did think, as I think now, that poverty is a weight about the neck of a public man. But I can say truthfully, that it was *your* ability to cope with it, rather than mine, that I feared."

"And it seems to me," said Pembroke, calmly, "on looking back, that I was a little too aggressive—that I put rather a forced construction on what you said—and that I was very angry."

"I was angry, too—and it has angered me every time I have thought of it in these six years, that I was made to appear mercenary, when I am far from it—that a mere want of tact and judgment should have marked me in your esteem—or anybody else's, for that matter—as a perfectly cold and calculating woman."

She was certainly very angry now.

"But if I was wrong," said Pembroke, in a low, clear voice—for he used the resources of his delightful voice on poor Olivia as he had done on many men and some women before—"I have paid the price. The humiliation and the pangs of six years ago were much—and then, the feeling that, after all, there was but one woman in the world for me—ah, Olivia, sometimes I think you do not know how deep is the hold you took upon me. You would have seen in all these years, that however I might try, I could not forget you."

Olivia was not implacable.

When they came in the house, the Colonel was come, and in a gale of good humor. He had, however, great fault to find with Pembroke's course. He was too conciliatory—too willing to forget the blood shed upon the battlefields of Virginia—and then and there they entered upon a political discussion which made the old-fashioned mirrors on the drawing-room wall ring again. The Colonel brought down his fist and raved. "By Jove, sir, this is intolerable. My black boy, Petrarch (Petrarch continued to be the Colonel's boy), knows more about the subject than you do; and he's the biggest fool I ever saw. I'll be hanged, sir, if your statements are worth refuting." Pembroke withstood the sortie gallantly, and at intervals charged the enemy in splendid style, reducing the Colonel to oaths and splutterings and despair.

Olivia sat in a low chair by the round mahogany table, on which the old-fashioned lamp burned softly, casting mellow lights and shades upon her graceful figure. Occasionally a faint smile played about her eyes—whereat Pembroke seemed to gain inspiration, and attacked the Colonel's theories with renewed vigor.

Upon the Colonel's invitation he remained all night—the common mode of social intercourse in Virginia. Next morning, the Colonel was ripe for argument. Pembroke, however, to his immense disgust, refused to enter the lists and spent the morning dawdling with Olivia in the garden. About noon, the Colonel, in a rage sent Petrarch after the renegades. Three times did he return without them. The fourth time Petrarch's patience was exhausted.

"Marse French, fur de Lord's sake come ter ole marse. He done got de sugar in de glasses, an' de ice cracked up, an' he fyarly stan'nin' on he hade. He got out all dem ole yaller *Richmun Exameters*, printed fo' de wah, an' he say he gwi' bust yo' argifyins' all ter pieces. He mighty obstroporous, an' you better come along."

To this pathetic appeal Pembroke at last responded. Olivia, with downcast face, walked by his side. The Colonel was very much worked up and "mighty discontemptuous," as Petrarch expressed it.

"This is the third time, sir—" he began to roar.

"Never mind, Colonel," replied Pembroke, laughing. "We will have a plenty of time to quarrel. Olivia has promised to marry me in the summer."

"By Gad, sir—"

"Have a cigar. Now, where did we leave off last night? Oh, the Virginia Resolutions of 1798."

D. APPLETON & CO.'S PUBLICATIONS.

BRER RABBIT PREACHES

ON THE PLANTATION. By JOEL CHANDLER HARRIS, author of "Uncle Remus." With 23 Illustrations by E. W. KEMBLE, and Portrait of the Author. 12mo. Cloth, $1.50.

The most personal and in some respects the most important work which Mr. Harris has published since "Uncle Remus." Many will read between the lines and see the autobiography of the author. In addition to the stirring incidents which appear in the story, the author presents a graphic picture of certain phases of Southern life which have not appeared in his books before. There are also new examples of the folk-lore of the negroes, which became classic when presented to the public in the pages of "Uncle Remus."

"The book is in the characteristic vein which has made the author so famous and popular as an interpreter of plantation character."—*Rochester Union and Advertiser.*

"Those who never tire of Uncle Remus and his stories—with whom we would be accounted—will delight in Joe Maxwell and his exploits."—*London Saturday Review.*

"Altogether a most charming book."—*Chicago Times.*

"Really a valuable, if modest, contribution to the history of the civil war within the Confederate lines, particularly on the eve of the catastrophe. While Mr. Harris, in his preface, professes to have lost the power to distinguish between what is true and what is imaginative in his episodical narrative, the reader readily finds the clew. Two or three new animal fables are introduced with effect; but the history of the plantation, the printing-office, the black runaways, and white deserters, of whom the impending break-up made the community tolerant, the coon and fox hunting, forms the serious purpose of the book, and holds the reader's interest from beginning to end. Like 'Daddy Jake,' this is a good anti slavery tract in disguise, and does credit to Mr. Harris's humanity. There are amusing illustrations by E. W. Kemble."—*New York Evening Post.*

"A charming little book, tastefully gotten up.... Its simplicity, humor, and individuality would be very welcome to any one who was weary of the pretentiousness and the dull obviousness of the average three-volume novel."—*London Chronicle.*

"The mirage of war vanishes and reappears like an ominous shadow on the horizon, but the stay-at-home whites of the Southern Confederacy were likewise threatened by fears of a servile insurrection. This dark dread exerts its influence on a narration which is otherwise cheery with boyhood's fortunate freedom from anxiety, and sublime disregard for what the morrow may bring forth. The simple chronicle of old times 'on the plantation' concludes all too soon; the fire burns low and the tale is ended just as the reader becomes acclimated to the mid-Georgian village, and feels thoroughly at home with Joe and Mink. The 'Owl and the Birds,' 'Old Zip Coon,' the 'Big Injun and the Buzzard,' are joyous echoes of the plantation-lore that first delighted us in 'Uncle Remus.' Kemble's illustrations, evidently studied from life, are interspersed in these pages of a book of consummate charm."—*Philadelphia Ledger.*

FROM DUSK TO DAWN. By KATHARINE P. WOODS, author of "Metzerott, Shoemaker." 12mo. Cloth, $1.25.

This book is an original one, like its predecessor, in that it follows none of the beaten paths of fiction, and it raises questions of vital interest, and addresses itself to the reader's thought instead of merely tickling his fancy. The influence of one human being over another is a subject of curious analysis, as well as the relation of the individual to the community, a subject, with its varied amplifications, which is of the first moment to-day. There is a story, a romance, which will interest novel-readers, but the book will hold the attention of those for whom the average novel has little charm.

GOD'S FOOL. A Koopstad Story. By MAARTEN MAARTENS, author of "Joost Avelingh." 12mo. Cloth, $1.25.

In the opinion of competent critics this new novel by Maarten Maartens represents the finest development thus far of the author's powers, and its appearance in book form promises to cause what is termed in popular parlance the "literary sensation" of the season. At least, there can be no question regarding the high appreciation of Maarten Maartens's work by American and English readers.

"Maarten Maartens is a capital story-teller."—*Pall Mall Gazette.*

"Maarten Maartens is a man who, in addition to mere talent, has in him a vein of genuine genius."—*London Academy.*

CAPT'N DAVY'S HONEYMOON. A Manx Yarn. By HALL CAINE, author of "The Deemster," "The Scape-Goat," etc. 12mo. Cloth, $1.00.

"A new departure by this author. Unlike his previous works, this little tale is almost wholly humorous, with, however, a current of pathos underneath. It is not always that an author can succeed equally well in tragedy and in comedy, but it looks as though Mr. Hall Caine would be one of the exceptions."—*London Literary World.*

"Constructed with great ingenuity. The story is full of delight."—*Boston Advertiser.*

"A rollicking story of Manx life, well told.... Mr. Caine has really written no book superior in character-drawing and dramatic force to this little comedy."—*Boston Beacon.*

FOOTSTEPS OF FATE. By LOUIS COUPERUS, author of "Eline Vere." Translated from the Dutch by Clara Bell. With an Introduction by Edmund Gosse. Holland Fiction Series. 12mo. Cloth, $1.00.

"It is a very remarkable book, and can not fail to make a profound impression by its strength and originality.... Its interest is intense, and the tragedy with which it closes is depicted with remarkable grace and passion."—*Boston Saturday Evening Gazette.*

"The dramatic development up to a tragical climax is in the manner of a true artist."—*Philadelphia Bulletin.*

THE FAITH DOCTOR. By EDWARD EGGLESTON, author of "The Hoosier Schoolmaster," "The Circuit Rider," etc., 12mo. Cloth, $1.50.

"One of *the* novels of the decade."—*Rochester Union and Advertiser.*

"It is extremely fortunate that the fine subject indicated in the title should have fallen into such competent hands."—*Pittsburgh Chronicle-Telegraph.*

"The author of 'The Hoosier Schoolmaster' has enhanced his reputation by this beautiful and touching study of the character of a girl to love whom proved a liberal education to both of her admirers."—*London Athenæum.*

"'The Faith Doctor' is worth reading for its style, its wit, and its humor, and not less, we may add, for its pathos."—*London Spectator.*

"Much skill is shown by the author in making these 'fads' the basis of a novel of great interest.... One who tries to keep in the current of good novel-reading must certainly find time to read 'The Faith Doctor.'"—*Buffalo Commercial.*

AN UTTER FAILURE. By MIRIAM COLES HARRIS, author of "Rutledge." 12mo. Cloth, $1.25.

"A story with an elaborate plot, worked out with great cleverness and with the skill of an experienced artist in fiction. The interest is strong and at times very dramatic.... Those who were attracted by 'Rutledge' will give hearty welcome to this story, and find it fully as enjoyable as that once immensely popular novel."—*Boston Saturday Evening Gazette.*

"In this new story the author has done some of the best work that she has ever given to the public, and it will easily class among the most meritorious and most original novels of the year."—*Boston Home Journal.*

"The author of 'Rutledge' does not often send out a new volume, but when she does it is always a literary event.... Her previous books were sketchy and slight when compared with the finished and trained power evidenced in 'An Utter Failure.'"—*New Haven Palladium.*

A PURITAN PAGAN. By JULIEN GORDON, author of "A Diplomat's Diary," etc. 12mo. Cloth, $1.00.

"Mrs. Van Rensselaer Cruger grows stronger as she writes.... The lines in her story are boldly and vigorously etched."—*New York Times.*

"The author's recent books have made for her a secure place in current literature, where she can stand fast.... Her latest production, 'A Puritan Pagan,' is an eminently clever story, in the best sense of the word clever."—*Philadelphia Telegraph.*

"It is obvious that the author is thoroughly at home in illustrating the manner and the sentiment of the best society of both America and Europe."—*Chicago Times.*

ELINE VERE. By LOUIS COUPERUS. Translated from the Dutch by J. T. GREIN. With an Introduction by EDMUND GOSSE. Holland Fiction Series. 12mo. Cloth, $1.00.

"Most careful in its details of description, most picturesque in its coloring."—*Boston Post.*

"A vivacious and skillful performance, giving an evidently faithful picture of society, and evincing the art of a true story-teller."—*Philadelphia Telegraph.*

"The *dénoûment* is tragical, thrilling, and picturesque."—*New York World.*

STRAIGHT ON. A story of a boy's school-life in France. By the author of "The Story of Colette." With 86 Illustrations by Edouard Zier. 320 pages. 8vo. Cloth, $1.50.

"It is long since we have encountered a story for children which we can recommend more cordially. It is good all through and in every respect."—*Charleston News and Courier.*

"A healthful tale of a French school-boy who suffers the usual school-boy persecution, and emerges from his troubles a hero. The illustrations are bright and well drawn, and the translation is excellently done."—*Boston Commercial Bulletin.*

"A real story-book of the sort which is difficult to lay down, having once begun it. It is fully illustrated and handsomely bound."—*Buffalo Courier.*

"The story is one of exceptional merit, and its delightful interest never flags."—*Chicago Herald.*

ILLUSTRATED EDITION OF "COLETTE."

THE STORY OF COLETTE, a new, large-paper edition. With 36 Illustrations. 8vo. Cloth, $1.50.

The great popularity which this book has attained in its smaller form has led the publishers to issue an illustrated edition, with thirty-six original drawings by Jean Claude, both vignette and full-page.

"This is a capital translation of a charming novel. It is bright, witty, fresh, and humorous. 'The Story of Colette' is a fine example of what a French novel can be, and all should be."—*Charleston News and Courier.*

"Colette is French and the story is French, and both are exceedingly pretty. The story is as pure and refreshing as the innocent yet sighing gayety of Colette's life."—*Providence Journal.*

"A charming little story, molded on the simplest lines, thoroughly pure, and admirably constructed. It is told with a wonderful lightness and raciness. It is full of little skillful touches, such as French literary art at its best knows so well how to produce. It is characterized by a knowledge of human nature and a mastery of style and method which indicate that it is the work rather of a master than of a novice.... Whoever the author of 'Colette' may be, there can be no question that it is one of the prettiest, most artistic, and in every way charming stories that French fiction has been honored with for a long time."—*New York Tribune.*

HERMINE'S TRIUMPHS. A Story for Girls and Boys. By MADAME COLOMB. With 100 Illustrations. 8vo. Cloth.

The popularity of this charming story of French home life, which has passed through many editions in Paris, has been earned by the sustained interest of the narrative, the sympathetic presentation of character, and the wholesomeness of the lessons which are suggested. One of the most delightful books for girls published in recent years. It is bound uniformly with "Straight On."